Radio Times

A musical

Music by Noel Gay

Book by Abi Grant

Book devised by Robin Miller
Original conception by Alex Armitage

Additional material and book revisions by
Paul Alexander and Alex Armitage

Samuel French — London
New York - Toronto - Hollywood

© 2002 BY ALEX ARMITAGE COMPANY LTD (BOOK)

This play is fully protected under the Copyright Laws of the British Commonwealth of Nations, the United States of America and all countries of the Berne and Universal Copyright Conventions.

All rights including Stage, Motion Picture, Radio, Television, Public Reading, and Translation into Foreign Languages, are strictly reserved.

No part of this publication may lawfully be reproduced in ANY form or by any means — photocopying, typescript, recording (including video-recording), manuscript, electronic, mechanical, or otherwise—or be transmitted or stored in a retrieval system, without prior permission.

SAMUEL FRENCH LTD, 52 FITZROY STREET, LONDON W1T 5JR, or their authorized agents, issue licences to amateurs to give performances of this play on payment of a fee. **This fee is subject to contract and subject to variation at the sole discretion of Samuel French Ltd.**

Licences for amateur performances are issued subject to the understanding that it shall be made clear in all advertising matter that the audience will witness an amateur performance; that the names of the authors of the plays shall be included on all programmes; and that the integrity of the authors' work will be preserved.

The publication of this play does not imply that it is necessarily available for performance by amateurs or professionals, either in the British Isles or Overseas. Amateurs and professionals considering a production are strongly advised in their own interests to apply to the appropriate agents for consent before starting rehearsals or booking a theatre or hall.

ISBN 0 573 08108 5

Page iv forms part of the Copyright information for this work and should be read in conjunction with the above notice

RADIO TIMES

First presented by Alex Armitage with Polygram Entertainment at the Birmingham Repertory Theatre on 8th September 1992. The production was subsequently presented by arrangement with Stoll Moss Theatres Ltd at the Queen's Theatre, London, on 15th October 1992 with the following cast:

Sammy Shaw	Tony Slattery
Wilfred Davies	Ian Bartholomew
Amy Chapman	Harriet Benson
Jeeps	James Buller
Olive James	Kathryn Evans
Heathcliffe Bultitude	Peter Rutherford
Gary Strong	Jeff Shankley
The Grosvenors	Helen Anker
	Linda Mae Brewer
	Kathy Norcross
	Tamzin Outhwaite
	Martin Eyre
	Ben Richards

Directed by David Gilmore
Sound design by Rick Clarke
Musical supervision and orchestrations by Chris Walker
Musical direction by Robert Scott
Executive producer David Cole
Lighting design by Paul Pyant
Set and costume design by Terry Parsons
Choreography and musical staging by Anthony Van Laast

Additional lyrics by Don Black and Chris Walker

"Turn On the Music" Lyrics by Noel Gay and Desmond Carter
Music by Noel Gay © 1931 by RA Ltd/Chappell Music
"La Di Da Di Da" Lyrics by Desmond Carter
Music by Noel Gay © 1934 by RA Ltd/Chappell Music
"You've Done Something to My Heart" Lyrics by Frank Eyton/Ian Grant
Music by Noel Gay © 1939 by Noel Gay Music
"Hey Little Hen" Lyrics by Noel Gay/Ralph Butler. Music by Noel Gay
© 1941 by Noel Gay Music/Campbell Connelly & Co Ltd
"Laughing at the Rain" Lyrics by Joseph Gilbert. Additional lyrics (1991) by
Chris Walker. Music by Noel Gay © 1931 by Noel Gay Music/EMI Music Pub
"Just One More" Lyrics by Noel Gay. Music by Noel Gay
© 1932 by RA Ltd/EMI Music Pub
"I Took My Harp to a Party" Lyrics by Desmond Carter
Music by Noel Gay © 1935 by RA Ltd/Chappell Music
"Hello to the Sun" Lyrics by Noel Gay/Frank Eyton. Music by Noel Gay
© 1942 by RA Ltd/Campbell Connelly & Co Ltd
"Let the People Sing" Lyrics by Frank Eyton/Ian Grant
Music by Noel Gay © 1939 by Noel Gay Music
"Oh, Buddy, I'm in Love" Lyrics by Noel Gay/Ralph Butler. Music by Noel Gay
© 1940 by Noel Gay Music/Campbell Connelly & Co Ltd
"Who's Been Polishing the Sun?" Lyrics by Noel Gay
Music by Noel Gay © 1934 by RA Ltd
"Someone Else" Lyrics by Don Black (formerly "Windsor Melody")
Music by Noel Gay © 1948 by Noel Gay Music
Military Medley:
"The King's Horses" Lyrics by Noel Gay/Harry Graham
Music by Noel Gay © 1930 by RA Ltd/Redwood Music Ltd
"The Fleet's in Port Again" Lyrics by Noel Gay
Music by Noel Gay © 1936 by RA Ltd
"There's Something About a Soldier" Lyrics by Noel Gay
Music by Noel Gay © 1933 by RA Ltd
"A Girl Who Loves a Soldier" Lyrics by Ralph Butler. Music by Noel Gay
© 1939 by Noel Gay/Campbell Connelly & Co Ltd
"Ali Baba's Camel" Lyrics by Noel Gay. Music by Noel Gay. © 1931 by RA Ltd
"Run, Rabbit, Run" Lyrics by Noel Gay/Ralph Butler. Music by Noel Gay
© 1939 by Noel Gay Music/Campbell Connelly & Co Ltd
"All for the Love of a Lady" Lyrics by Archie Gotler
Music by Noel Gay ©   by Noel Gay Music/EMI Music
"I'm Sending My Blessings" Lyrics by Noel Gay/Joe Lubin/Joseph Gilbert.
Music by Noel Gay © 1944 by Noel Gay Music
"My Thanks to You" Lyrics by Norman Newell
Music by Noel Gay © 1950 by Noel Gay Music
"Song of Tomorrow" by Noel Gay/Hugh Charles/Sonny Miller
© 1944 by Noel Gay Music

MUSICAL NUMBERS

Overture

ACT I

1	**Turn On the Music** (Olive, Wilf, Jeeps, Amy & All)
2	**La Di Da Di Da** (Wilf, Olive, Sammy & All)
3	**You've Done Something to My Heart** (Jeeps)
4	**Hey Little Hen** (Wilf, Grosvenors)
5	**Laughing at the Rain** (Wilf)
6	**Just One More** (Gary, Olive)
7	**I Took My Harp to a Party** (Bultitude)
8	**Hello to the Sun** (Wilf, Olive, Amy, Bultitude, Sammy & All)
9	**Let the People Sing** (All)
10	**Oh Buddy I'm in Love** (Gary)
11	**Who's Been Polishing the Sun** (Sammy, Grosvenors)
11A	**Who's Been Polishing the Sun** Reprise (Sammy & Grosvenors)

Entr'acte

ACT II

12	**Someone Else** (Olive)
12A	**Someone Else** Reprise (Olive)
13	**Military Medley : The King's Horses/The Fleet's in Port/There's Something About a Soldier/A Girl Who Loves a Soldier** (Olive, Amy & Grosvenors)
14	**Ali Baba's Camel** (Sammy, Wilf, Bultitude, Band & All)
15	**Run, Rabbit, Run** (Grosvenors)
16	**All for the Love of a Lady** (Grosvenors, Olive, Bultitude, Band & All)
17	**I'm Sending My Blessings** (Amy, Grosvenors)
18	**A Song of Tomorrow** (Sammy, Grosvenors & All)
19	**My Thanks to You** (Sammy)
20	**A Song of Tomorrow** Reprise (Sammy, Olive, Wilf, Jeeps, Bultitude, Gary & All)
21	**The Calls** (Sammy & All)

The music for *Radio Times* is available on hire from Samuel French Ltd.

AUTHOR BILLING REQUIREMENTS

All producers of RADIO TIMES *must* give credit to the AUTHORS of the Work in all programmes distributed in connection with performances of the Work, and in all instances in which the title of the Work appears for the purposes of advertising, publicizing or otherwise exploiting a production thereof; including, without limitation to, programmes, souvenir books and playbills.

Billing must be substantially as follows:

Music by Noel Gay — 100%

Book by Abi Grant — 75%

Book devised by Robin Miller — 50%
Original conception by Alex Armitage — 50%

Additional material and book revisions by
Paul Alexander and Alex Armitage — 75%

CHARACTERS

Sammy Shaw: *very successful radio star, has his own show. Think Tommy Hanley/Arthur Askey; 35-50*
Wilfred Davies: *Sammy's sidekick, older than Sammy. Many years on the halls. The rock on which Sammy's genius can build; 45+*
Amy Chapman: *gorgeous soubrette, think Jesse Matthews/Vera Lynn. The Radio Girl Friend, sweetheart of everyone in uniform; 18-25*
Jeeps: *the sound effects man/studio producer, responsible/ gets blamed for everything. Surprisingly young and a genius at creating atmosphere and sound effects in the studio, extremely handsome; 20-30*
Olive James: *Sammy's long-suffering other-half, a veteran of music halls, singer/comedienne. Very glamorous and stylish, would have married Sammy a long time ago*
Heathcliffe Bultitude: *BBC staff producer, would be much happier producing cultural music and arts programmes, not showbusiness at all. Immaculately suited and highly polished; 45+*
Gary Strong: *English, went to Hollywood and became a huge movie star, think David Niven/Clark Gable. Very smooth and sophisticated, has own suntan; 35-45*
The Grosvenors (including **Simon**, **Andrew**, **Irene**, **Daisy**, **Sophie**): *the all-singing, all-dancing back-up group. Provide the glamour, the harmonies and anything else that's needed. Although great at their jobs it must be remembered that none of the Grosvenors has been called up into military service*

The action takes place before, during and after a live radio transmission from the Criterion Theatre, London.

The Criterion Theatre was used for broadcasting because of its wholly underground location. Very often the cast and crew would stay in the theatre overnight if raids meant they could not get home.

Time — Spring 1941

VARIETY BANDWAGON

SAMMY SHAW

Star of the show, Sammy Shaw, has come a long way since his first appearance on a music hall stage at the age of seventeen. Mr Shaw's first radio appearance was on *Laughing and Joking with the Boys* in 1934 and he graduated to his own show in 1939. His films include *Tondeleyo, Portsmouth Adventure, Whoops-a-Daisy!, Variety Jubilee*, alongside the Ganjou Brothers and Juanita, and *Music Hath Charms*. His latest picture, *I'm Doing It Too!*, will be released later this year.

OLIVE JAMES

A star of Mr C.B. Cochrane's and Mr Andre Charlot's revues. Miss James is well-known as "the girl in the yellow dress", singer of the popular song "Just One More". She played for over a year in the hit West End musical *Me and My Girl*, starring opposite Lupino Lane. Miss James first worked with Sammy Shaw in variety, followed by *Whoops-a-Daisy!*. She is also featured in the soon -to-be-released *"I'm Doing It Too!.*

AMY CHAPMAN

Miss Chapman began her career as a dancer in Mr C.B. Cochrane's revues. She has enjoyed performing as a singer with bandleaders such as Ambrose, Jack Hylton and, most successfully, with Carroll Gibbons and the Savoy Hotel Orpheans at the Savoy Hotel in London and on many radio broadcasts. She was spotted by Sammy in 1942 and has been the Variety Bandwagon "Radio Girl Friend" ever since.

GARY STRONG

Well-known as the star of *Pot o'Gold, Kiss the Boys Goodbye* and *Second Chorus*, in which he played opposite Fred Astaire, Gary Strong got his first break in movies in 1936 in the hit musical comedy, *Husband's Vacation*. This followed four months as a stuntman for Warner Brothers and two years touring the United States as a dance band singer. His own hugely successful cabaret act has enjoyed engagements at the Moulin Rouge and in Las Vegas.

WILFRED DAVIES

Mr Davies' music hall career began in 1929 with a piano, song and dialogue act in his home town of Bristol. His double act with Sammy Shaw ("The Men With Extremely Baggy Trousers") evolved from a guest appearance they made on *The Roosters*. His only film appearance to date has been in *Music Hath Charms*, which featured his farmyard animal impressions. He was also honoured to have the opportunity of performing these at the Royal Variety Performance in 1938.

MR BULTITUDE

A graduate in geography from Manchester University, Mr Bultitude spent five months as a seminary student before hearing the call of radio. He joined the BBC in 1934. Specialising in outside broadcasts, he has worked on Test Matches from the Oval, as well as numerous news broadcasts and gardening programmes. His proudest moment came when he assisted on the broadcast of the Coronation of King George VI in 1937.

ALAN PATTERSON

Our radio ventriloquist began his career in variety with his Alan "what cold hands you have" Patterson act (sadly curtailed at the request of the Lord Chamberlain). After a brief spell away, he joined the merchant navy, where he became a favourite at entertaining his shipmates. He returned to dry land to join the chorus of *Chu Chin Chow*, but a chance meeting with a dummy led him to develop his skills as a ventriloquist. In his spare time he runs an antique business in Maida Vale. "Mind your beeswax, Mr Patterson!" says dummy Andy.

These programme notes may be freely used for the purposes of advertising and promotion of amateur productions.

ACT I

Overture

The stage of the Criterion Theatre, London. Spring 1941

The stage is set with the normal details of a rehearsal: baskets, rehearsal piano SR *(behind tabs line), tea urn* US, *costumes, a ventriloquist's doll, chairs etc.. There is a sound effects table* DSL *(front of tabs), above the table is an "On Air" sign, and green/red studio lights. The band are hidden on one or both sides of the stage. Wilf picks out a tune on the piano as Olive (wearing a big fur coat), Amy, Jeeps and the Grosvenors enter and rehearse the song as they prepare for performance. By the end of the song all are together choreographed into a routine, with Jeeps at his sound effects table. After the song the Grosvenors exit/enter as required. They prepare for the show, rehearse, try on costumes, drink tea etc.*

No. 1: Turn On the Music

Olive
I don't deal in slow tunes
Give me heel and toe tunes
I want a chance
To jump up and dance
To something with rhythm and swing.

Wilf
I hate dull and dry things
Dreamy lullaby things
Cut the gavotte stuff
Give me the hot stuff
Thrill me with that sort of thing.

All
Turn on the music
Let's have some music
The sort of music
That we can shout about
Turn on a glad song
A raving mad song
If it's a sad song
We'll cut it out.

	We want to sing the chorus The night's before us The things that bore us have gone So while we've got time We'll have a hot time If we can keep the music turned on.
Jeeps	When infatuation Hears that syncopation Though love is blind you Soon are inclined to Throw back your shoulders and sing.
Amy	If yours is a blue tune Find yourself a new tune We want a chance To jump up and dance To something by Hylton or Bing.
All	Turn on the music Let's have some music The sort of music That we can shout about.

Wilf Ladies and gentlemen — welcome to "Variety Bandwagon", the flagship of the BBC's radio output! So just think what the rest of the fleet must look like!

All	Turn on a glad tune A raving mad tune If it's a sad tune We'll cut it out. We want to sing the chorus The night's before us The things that bore us have gone. So while we've got time We'll have a hot time If we can keep the music turned on If you think Brahms distressing Or find Tchaikovsky too depressing Keep the music turned on.

Act I 3

The music resumes under

Wilf And now, the star of our show — he is to radio comedy what Hitler is to Poland. A man renowned for his comic timing. Four hours to read *The Beano*. He's a national treasure — people are always asking where we dug him up — ladies and gentlemen, the one, the thankfully only, *Mister Sammy "I'm-Doing-It" Shawwwwwww!*

The music swells. A spotlight shines on SR *and* ——

Nothing. Not a dickybird. The music starts to fade and dies. The spotlight wanders around the stage, searching for a star. The Grosvenors gravitate around the tea urn. Finally it alights on a small doorway at the back of the stage. The door opens

Bultitude comes through it. Far from happy

Bultitude Where is he?
Olive (*innocently*) Who?
Bultitude Where's Shaw?
Wilf Where's my what?
Bultitude Not "your" — *Shaw*! Sammy Shaw! Our — for want of a better word — star!
Wilf Oh. Him. He — um — he …
Olive He — popped out.
Bultitude Popped out? Popped out! But tonight is the most important night in Home Service history! Tonight we give the public something they've never before heard on the BBC.
Wilf You mean entertainment?
Bultitude A *live* broadcast to the United States! Of America! This is our chance to impress upon all Americans that we are a nation of courage. Of moral fortitude. A small but completely unflappable race. (*Flapping*) AND WE GO ON AIR IN LESS THAN THREE HOURS! WE MUST FIND HIM!

Bultitude strides purposefully into the wings, SL

Olive (*anxiously*) Wilf — where is he?
Wilf Well, I checked all the pubs — all the bookies …
Olive Any luck?
Wilf No. And I didn't find Sammy either. You must have some idea, Olive. After all — he does live with you!
Olive Just pops by every now and then to visit his toothbrush. And he didn't come home last night!

Bultitude appears from the wings SL, *highly agitated*

Bultitude Oh this is too much. Too much! Shaw!

He strides into the wings SR

Olive He didn't even telephone. And the raids last night were awful. Oh Wilf, if he's been killed — I'll murder him.

Wilf comforts her as Bultitude reappears from the wings SR

Bultitude That's it. Mr Shaw has made a fool of me for the last time. Do you understand?
Olive Yes. Whose turn is it now?
Bultitude I'm calling the Director General of the BBC. And if he's at lunch I'm calling the Home Office!

Wilf and Olive exchange an alarmed look — then Wilf swings Bultitude around and pushes him on to a chair

Wilf Mr B, don't take on so ... This is a comedy show. And you know the one thing you need to do comedy?
Bultitude A *comedian*?
Wilf An *attitude*. I mean, Sammy may be our star, but you're our *producer*! So get an attitude. Like us — gay, happy, carefree ...

No. 2: La Di Da Di Da

He gestures to the Grosvenors — none of whom look remotely gay, happy or carefree. They snap change into forced grins

Wilf   If you start the day
              Without a smile
              Your food is indigestible
              And life looks vile
              And you'll have spots
              Dancing before your eyes.

Bultitude Yes, yes, yes. But I still haven't seen a script.
Wilf And I've never seen Santa Claus. But I believe in my heart he exists!

              There is still one ray
              Of hope for you

Act I 5

>Though everything's detestable
>The whole day through
>I'll tell you what's
>Certain to clear the skies.

Bultitude tries to get up but Olive sits on his lap to stop him

Olive Try a little deep breathing
You'll find it will help you along
Take a deep breath — hold it —
Then burst into song.

Wilf If you crawl out of bed
And you feel nearly dead
And you think you'll be sick
And you are
Try this — (*He breathes in*)
La di da di da di da di da.

If you've corns on your feet
And you can't get a seat
On a bus or a train or a car
Try this — (*He breathes in*)
La di da di da di da di da.

Rise on your toes
Turn to the south
In through the nose
Out through the mouth.

If you're tired of your life
And your work and your wife
And your clothes and your kids
And your car
Try this — (*He breathes in*)
La di da di da di da di da.

Bultitude snaps. The music stops. Sharp

Bultitude Stop! I know what you're doing and it won't work! Mr Shaw has taken his last liberty! As of 4 p.m. this afternoon, he is no longer employed by the BBC!

Olive But — you can't just sack Sammy!

Bultitude I'm not, Miss James. By not being here, Sammy will be sacking himself — unless he can make it in (*he looks at his watch*) ten seconds.

They all gather round Bultitude's watch

    Sammy enters from behind them, wearing crumpled full evening gear and top hat. He is carrying a script — a mess of papers

Sammy Ten seconds? Ten seconds? In ten seconds I can make it twice and still have time for a cigarette.
Olive Sammy!

Sammy kisses her on the cheek

Sammy There'll never be another.

    If you're tired of your life
    And your work and your wife
    And your clothes and your kids
    And your car
    Try this — (*He breathes in*)
    La di da di da di da di da.

(*To Bultitude*)   Rise on your toes
    Turn to the south
    In through the nose
    Out through the mouth.

    If you get rather stout
    And your hair's falling out
    And you feel twice as old as you are
    Try this — (*He breathes in*)
    La di da di da di da di da.

    Time to rejoice
    Don't be depressed
    Lift up your voice
    Throw out your chest.

He puts his arm round Olive

    If you've been out all night
    And your girl wants a fight
    And you think you'll be caught
    And you are, try this — (*He breathes in*)

Act I

All La di da di da di da di
La di da di da di da di
La di da di da di da di
La di da di da
La di da di da
La di da di da di da di
La di da di da.

La di da di da di da di
La di da di da
La di da di da
La di da di da di da di
La di da di da.

La di da di da di da di
La di da di da
La di da di da
La di da di da di da di
La di da di da di da di da.

Jeeps exits

Olive Sammy! Why didn't you phone? It was a bad raid last night. A lot of people got hit in the docks.
Sammy Well, don't you worry love — my docks are fine. Come here.

Jeeps enters

Jeeps Mr Bultitude — telephone!
Bultitude (*taking fright*) The Home Office?
Jeeps Well they had a deep, gruff, angry voice.
Bultitude (*relaxing*) Ah no. That must be my wife.

Bultitude exits

Sammy (*grabbing a tea*) All right you lot, there's a show to put on. Back to whatever you were doing before we were so rudely Luftwaffed.

They start to bustle

Come on! Rehearse! I want to see a show full of glamour and music. Of song, dance and sparkling repartee …
Simon And so you shall … (*He holds out a half crown*)

Sammy What's this? Two and six?
Simon Enough for a stalls seat at the Palladium.
Sammy (*taking the money*) Simon, however much they're paying you — it's more than your IQ.

Simon rejoins the other Grosvenors. The Grosvenors huddle around sheet music. With company energy levels restored, Sammy slumps in a corner with Wilf

Wilf Sammy — can I give you a word of advice?
Sammy If it's another racing tip — no. I can't afford it.
Wilf It's about Olive. Olive is — well, she's special. In fact, she loves you, so she's more than special — she's insane. The least you could do is go home sometimes.
Sammy I was on my way home. I was at the *Savoy*.
Wilf And the trains to Windsor run from the *Savoy* now do they?
Sammy I wanted to finish off or start off the script so I just popped in to use the facilities.
Wilf The cocktail bar facilities.
Sammy Of course. And I got talking to Noël and one Martini led to another and before I knew it, I was up in my suite writing this week's script. I didn't get on a train 'cos I can't write on trains — they move.
Wilf And you lost the ability to use a phone?
Sammy I was going to phone Olive but we got bombed into the shelter.
Wilf She was dead worried, you know Sammy.
Sammy Yes, well Olive likes to worry. Takes her mind off her problems. (*He groans*)
Wilf The Martinis are awake. How d'you feel?
Sammy You know how you feel when you've been up all night drinking cheap beer and chain smoking?
Wilf Yes.
Sammy I wish I felt that good.
Sammy }
Wilf } (*together*) I thank yew.
Wilf How's the script? Nothing cheap, I hope?
Sammy *Cheap*! Are you suggesting I pay for this stuff? Two things I have never paid for — sex and jokes. Which, coincidentally, are the two I get the biggest laughs doing. (*He raises his cup of tea and deliberately bumps it against his forehead*)

Irene enters

Oops! I thought I was taller.

Act I

Irene hands Sammy a note

Irene This was at the stage door.
Sammy Ta.
Irene Pleasure, treasure.
Sammy (*pained*) Ah! (*He points at the ventriloquist's doll*) It's from Patterson. Mile End Station was hit last night and he's trying to cadge a lift in. Dammit! Bloody Nazis! First France, then Poland, now the ventriloquist!

Bultitude enters

Bultitude Mr Shaw!
Sammy Mr Bultitude!

Sammy hands Bultitude the script

Bultitude This should have been handed in yesterday.
Sammy I know, but — don't tell anyone — there's a war on.
Bultitude (*taking a green form out and waving it vigorously under Sammy's nose*) Have you done this?
Sammy Not in public. People would talk.
Bultitude Have I had your breakdown?
Sammy No, but it's very kind of you to offer.
Bultitude (*losing patience*) Mr Shaw, as you know very well indeed, all BBC programmes must submit a contents breakdown to the Home Office ——
Sammy Before transmission. For security clearance. Yes, I know. Very well. Indeed.
Bultitude Failure to comply means cancellation — even mid-broadcast!
Wilf And there's nothing worse than having your plug pulled in the middle.
Sammy I handed it in this morning. The red tapeworms have it as we speak. Sammy Shaw is nothing if not professional.
Bultitude I have never seen any evidence of that.
Sammy And I've never seen my father — but I know in my heart he exists.
Bultitude And what about tonight's guest star?
Sammy Ah-ha! (*He jumps on a chair*) Ladies and gentlemen, friends, fellow professionals, and you Mr Bultitude ...

They all gather round

As befits the historic nature of tonight's broadcast, our guest is a huge star. Currently resident at the *Savoy* before joining up with the RAF. Massive — unforgettable (*he clutches his brow*) — oh, what's his name ... ?
Grosvenors Come on. Tell us! etc. ...

Sammy You've heard of Cary Grant. You've heard of Clark Gable — Well, he's heard of them too. In fact, he's played dominoes with them, because — he's — *Gary Strong!*

The Grosvenors applaud. Olive seems mysteriously shaken. She gently tugs on Sammy's sleeve

Olive *The* Gary Strong?
Sammy Accept no imitations.

She melts to one side pensively

Wilf Sammy — you could talk the devil into going to church.
Sammy No, no. He's over to join up. He heard the show and asked to be on it.
Wilf Heard the show and *asked* to be on it? Has he had his medical?
Amy Gary Strong is coming here! How wonderful!

The girls in the Grosvenors and Amy get steadily more excited and carried away

Daisy He's sooooo good-looking ...
Amy But, classy ...
Sophie His voice ...
Amy His walk ...
Irene His *legs* ...
Amy And those eyes! Why he's just the most gorgeous man alive!

As their passion rises, so does the boys' huffiness. They (including Wilf and Sammy) turn as one and make as if to exit

Boys Hurumph! Yeah, yeah, yeah *etc.*
Amy *(catching herself)* And of course he's a talented and versatile actor.
Bultitude I must check this script. *(Pointedly)* Let's just hope Strong isn't late!

Bultitude exits

With him gone, Sammy crosses to the piano and takes out a security clearance form and pen

Wilf Ungrateful so-and-so. I mean Gary Strong, that's what I call ... (*He*

Act I

turns and sees the form) A security clearance form! Sammy, you idiot! You said you'd done it.
Sammy Yes. But there's a perfectly good explanation for that.
Wilf What?
Sammy I lied. But there's still time. (*He checks the clock*) Just. People sing, adlib, adlib, joke, adlib, viz biz, adlib.
Wilf If Bultitude finds out ...
Sammy I'll know you told him. So shh ... (*He starts filling in the form*)
Wilf When does Mr Hollywood arrive?
Sammy Any minute. I hope he throws himself into the show.

Gary Strong enters at the back, spies Olive standing to one side, goes right up and hugs her

Trouble with those bigshot Yanks is they're so stand-offish. Never get involved with the cast. They turn up, but they're cold — distant — like they don't really want to know ...
Wilf (*clocking the embrace*) Er— Sammy ...
Sammy Quiet! You know I can't write and think at the same time.
Wilf But Sammy ...
Sammy What? (*He turns and sees too. He frowns and goes over to Olive and Gary*) Er — excuse me? Hello? Are there still two of you in there?

Gary and Olive part — Olive looking slightly flustered, embarrassed

Gary Hi Sammy. Great party last night. How is the head?
Sammy (*sarcastically*) Gary — Olive. Olive — Gary.
Gary We've met.
Sammy Met? You've *coalesced*.

Gary spots the form Sammy's holding. Absentmindedly he takes it and signs it (through the play, we see Gary's an inveterate autograph signer; whenever he sees a scrap of paper, script etc., his first and unconscious reaction is to sign it)

Olive I'm — old friends with Gary Strong. Or Gary Johnson as he used to be.

The Grosvenors are impressed

Gary (*handing back the form*) Hello everyone. I've heard so much about you. I'm looking forward to the show, I hope I'm not late. I can see I've kept you waiting.

Olive Some more than others.
Sammy (*a beat*) Old — friends?
Gary But now I'm here, can I just say what a pleasure it is?
Wilf Mmmm. I enjoy it too.
Sammy How — "old"?
Olive We did the halls together.
Gary Don't tell me you kept "Johnson and James" a secret? We weren't all that bad!
Olive We weren't great.
Gary We had our moments. Remember Glasgow? The blind seal trainer? We taped a herring to his underpants?

They laugh and embrace. A private joke. Sammy is stonefaced

Olive (*seeing Sammy's expression*) Maybe you had to be there ...
Sammy (*coughing; then casually*) When you say "friends" ...

Bultitude enters

Bultitude What's going on? What's the hold up?
Olive Mr Bultitude, this is Gary Strong ...

Wilf can't help winding Sammy up

Wilf They're old friends.
Bultitude How do you do, I'm the show's producer.

Gary shakes Bultitude's hand

Gary Congratulations. I don't like work either!

Everyone sniggers, except Bultitude of course

> No, seriously, nice to meet you, I'm looking forward to the show. And can I just say — it gives me great pleasure!

The others laugh. Bultitude doesn't get it

Olive Gary, let me quickly introduce you to the rest of the family ...

This turns into a tussle between Olive and Sammy, desperate to re-gain the initiative

> This is Amy ...

Act I

Sammy Our Radio Girl Friend.
Gary Lucky radio ...

He throws Amy a charming smile, much to Jeeps' agony

Olive Jeeps ...
Sammy Our talented and versatile sound engineer. (*He cups his hands to his mouth*) Say hello, Jeeps!
Jeeps (*sulkily*) Hello.
Sammy Our vocal back-up — they're vocal and they put everyone's back up — the Grosvenors ...
Gary Hi!
Grosvenors (*in harmony; rising major arpeggio sustained as chord*)) Hello, hello, hello, hello, hello ...
Daisy Oh, Mr Strong — I've seen all your films!
Gary Thank you. So have I.
Olive Over there — that's Monty Montgomery and his Getting Smaller All The Time Band ...
Gary Getting Smaller?
Sammy Enlistment.
Gary (*taking a look*) See what you mean — I've smoked cigars that had bigger bands.

General mirth — except for Sammy. Wilf stands, waiting to be introduced. But Sammy has other ideas. He claps his hands

Sammy Save it for the show. We're running out of time. Olive, take Wilf and find out the latest on the ventriloquist — Amy you look after Gary, make him feel at home — put shelves up and argue or something.
Wilf Hey! You haven't introduced me! Gary doesn't know who I am!
Sammy Lucky bloody Gary. (*To the others*) You lot — make yourselves useful, if anyone needs me, I'll be in a panic. And if I'm not there, I'll be in a dither.

All exit except Amy, Jeeps, and Gary

Gary and Amy sit. Jeeps stays behind them mimicking Gary's smoothness, and Amy's winsomeness. Jealous, it makes him sick

Gary So Miss Chapman, tell me all about yourself?
Amy (*thinking*) I'm single ... (*she gives a shy laugh*)
Gary Anything else?
Amy Did I mention I was single?

Gary Twice. And I found it even harder to believe the second time.
Amy Oh — Mr Strong ...
Gary Call me Gary ...
Amy Only if you call me Amy ...
Gary I'd be charmed to — Amy.

She giggles. Jeeps mimes this, but is caught at it as they turn

Amy Jeeps! Would you be an angel and run down to the office and pick up my mail. Mmm? Thank you.

Jeeps knows he's been got rid of and begins to exit slowly

The lights change, Gary and Amy freeze

Jeeps sings, taking Amy and dancing with her

No. 3: You've Done Something to My Heart

Jeeps   In my heart you've lit a flame
Since we met it's not the same
Since that fleeting yet fateful meeting
I keep repeating your name
Strange enchantment when you're with me
Desolation when you go
Is it love that you have brought me
Seems to me it must be so ...

You've done something to my heart
Some strange something to my heart
When we meet
Even in the street
I fear you'll hear the beat of my heart.

And every moment I'm with you
Holds a thrill I never knew
While you're there
There's magic in the air
That's never there whenever we're apart
For you've done something
Something to my heart!

While you're there
There's magic in the air

Act I

> That's never there whenever we're apart
> For you've done something
> Something to my heart!

Jeeps dances Amy back to not quite her original position with Gary. The spell breaks. Jeeps is embarrassed

Sammy marches on apoplectic, carrying song sheets

Sammy Where the devil are you? Wilf, whoever she is, put her down. Everybody here — now!
Gary Is anything wrong.
Sammy Wrong? Wrong!

Olive and Wilf rush on

Wilf What is it?
Olive What's happened?
Sammy It's — It's — oh, I can hardly bear to think about it! What a waste — what a terrible, shocking *waste*!
Olive Sammy, what is it?
Sammy We've lost another three minutes from the show!
Olive Is that all! The way you were going on, I'd thought the invasion had started!
Sammy No — this is serious! Your French maid has been cut.
Olive *What*?
Sammy Apparently she's "too sexy"!
Olive That's ridiculous!
Sammy I know. The way you play her she's funny. Any news on Patterson the ventriloquist?
Wilf Not a gleeding word.
Sammy Damn! Well I was saving this for next week's show. Let's run through it and see how it goes.

He hands around the song sheets. Gary takes one, absentmindedly signs it and returns it to Irene

Irene (*puzzled*) Thank you.
Sammy Jeeps, time it and sound-FX it as much as you can. We're looking for three minutes.
Jeeps Right.
Sammy OK everybody, places please.
Amy Anything I can do?

Gary Or me?

Sammy No, take five, we'll call you when we need you. All right Wilf, from the top.

Amy and Gary exit

Wilf takes position with his ukulele. The Grosvenors play the chickens in an extraordinary manner (chicken walking, wings flapping etc.)

No. 4: Hey Little Hen

Wilf I had a lot of chickens
A large chicken run

Sammy Try it Northern, Wilf, a Northern accent ...

Wilf (*ignoring Sammy*) I had a lot of chickens (*continuing*)
Sammy No, no, Northern England ...

Wilf A large chicken run
But owing to conditions
I'm now down to one
I give her lots of titbits
The dear little thing
And just to keep her up to scratch
I go to her and sing ....

Hey little hen, (*Bor Wuk*)
When, when, when,
Will you lay me an egg for my tea (*Buk Buk Buk Buk*)
Hey little hen (*Brrr (roll r) Uk*)
When, when, when,
Will you try to supply one for me? (*Buk Buk-Kah*)
Get into your nest (*Brrrrrr*)
Do your little best (*Buk*)
Get it off your chest (*Buk Buk*)
I can do the rest (*Buk Buk-Kah*)
Hey little hen (*Bor-Wuk*)
When, (*Buk*) when, (*Buk*) when, (*Buk*)
Will you lay me an egg for my tea? (*Clucking*)
Will you lay me an egg for my tea? (*Clucking*)

Sammy Well that was — it's hard to find the words really. That was ...

Act I

He looks to Jeeps

Jeeps Two minutes twenty?
Sammy Perfect! That's what it was. Repeat the chorus and we've got it. Go away and learn it.

Bultitude enters carrying a green book of guidelines as the Grosvenors exit

Bultitude What's that?
Sammy (*handing Bultitude a song sheet*) A filler for the French maid.
Wilf I thang yew!

Bultitude having scanned the lyrics hands the sheet back to Sammy

Bultitude Unacceptable!
Sammy What?
Bultitude Mr Shaw, I am here to look for vice and smut!
Wilf We have so much in common!
Bultitude Do you know what this is? (*He holds up the book*)
Sammy The Variety and Light Entertainment Official Guidelines, yes.
Bultitude Have you read it?
Sammy Couldn't put it down.
Bultitude And yet you claim to have no idea what I'm talking about? (*He thrusts the book at Sammy*) There.
Sammy (*reading*) "There is an absolute ban on jokes about or suggestive references to — fig leaves, lavatories, ladies underwear e.g., winter drawers on, rabbits, lodgers, commercial travellers, effeminacy in men ——"
Bultitude No, not there, there!
Sammy "There is an absolute ban upon jokes about immorality of any kind!"
Wilf Tell me Mr B, burnt any good books lately?
Bultitude The song. What was it about?
Sammy It was about two minutes twenty.
Bultitude Eggs! The song was about *eggs*.
Sammy But eggs aren't immoral!
Bultitude But they are rationed, and this could seriously damage morale! And where does low morale lead?

Sammy and Wilf look nonplussed

I'll tell you! To low morals! You start by allowing light-hearted songs about chickens and end up with jokes about God, sex and the Royal Family. Sex and the Royal Family! Then where would we be?
Wilf Windsor?

Sammy Come on, Mr B! Give us a bit of leeway. Where's your compassion?
Wilf Where's your milk of human kindness?
Sammy That's rationed as well.
Bultitude It's no use appealing to my better nature, Mr Shaw. Because this *is* my better nature.
Sammy Mr Bultitude. I've already lost Patterson the vent act, without Lou-Lou or the hen song I'm six minutes short. What shall I do?
Bultitude Don't ask me. I'm not a creative person I'm a producer. I suggest you do — something else. And do it quickly!

Bultitude exits

Sammy If you want me I'll be in the green room.
Wilf Doing what?
Sammy "Something else". *(He part exits, then turns)* Oh and Olive love ...?
Olive Yes?
Sammy This isn't the bloody Windmill you know, you are allowed to move!

He exits with a slam

A moment's silence, while Olive gives Wilf a long-suffering look

Wilf He's under a lot of pressure ...
Olive He will be when I drop the bloody piano on him.
Wilf He barks at me too, remember. Yesterday he said if our boys fought the way I sang we might as well surrender. You mustn't take his personal insults personally.
Olive Wilf ...
Wilf Yes?
Olive What do you do when the romance goes out of a relationship?
Wilf I get dressed and go home.
Olive Seriously.
Wilf Seriously, my mum always said the secret of a good relationship was to talk through all the big problems, and then bicker about everything else. Oh and remember the good times.
Olive Like our wedding for example?
Wilf Sammy meant to be with you on your wedding day, he just got caught up ...
Olive With a show, yes, I remember. Just for once, couldn't he have put me first? I needed him there ...
Wilf You needed a commitment ...
Olive Sod commitment! I'd forgotten to wear something old, borrowed and blue. I needed a copy of his act to tuck into my garter ...

Act I

Wilf laughs. Olive smiles a sad smile

Wilf You've put up with him for twelve years by seeing his funny side.
Olive The funny side I like. Trouble is, it seems to be his only side. Even a stamp has two ...
Wilf So — you want to see his sticky side?
Olive Sure. His sticky side. Or how about his romantic side? His happy side? His carefree side? His vulnerable side?
Wilf That's a lot of sides ...
Olive A man should have a lot of sides. Or is that a polyhedron? (*She sighs*) Look at me Wilf. I'm not getting any younger. I'd like a family. I'd like to be married. Not necessarily in that order.
Wilf And so would Sammy — I'm sure. He's just got other things on his mind.
Olive Yes. How do I compete with this show? With a *war*? Storm clouds may have gathered over Europe but do they all have to be billeted in my love life?
Wilf You just have to bear with him, Olive. And laugh with him.

No. 5: Laughing at the Rain

Storm clouds can't conceal
What you alone can heal
He may not show it
But you really know it's true.

Rain is falling fast ...
But it cannot last
You'll see the rain go
You'll see the rainbow too.

Smile a while and stop repining
Better times will come again
Till the sun commences shining
Just keep laughing at the rain.

Don't forget each new tomorrow
Though today drives you insane
Bide your time and hide your sorrow
Just keep laughing at the rain.

Take a tip from me
Use philosophy
Life is just what you make it

> Someday you'll be glad
> That you had my advice
> So take it.
>
> Then you'll see a silver lining
> Better times will come again
> Till the sun commences shining
> Just keep laughing at the rain
> Till the sun commences shining
> Just keep laughing at the rain.

Sammy loves you Olive, needs you too.
Olive Maybe you're right — he is special!

Sammy enters furious. They jump

Sammy Oi! You two layabouts! No, no. (*Sarcastic*) Don't get up. It's only ninety minutes to broadcast, we're short on material, a cast member is missing, our producer is quite possibly Adolf Hitler's grandad, but you leave everything to me. In fact I've got a spare fifteen seconds, I could get you some tea and cakes!
Wilf One sugar in mine please.
Olive Where are you going?
Sammy To see Bultitude. I feel a tantrum coming on. (*He mimes strangling Bultitude*)
Olive (*exasperated*) Sammy this may come as a surprise to you — but some people don't like being shouted at. They respond badly. So why don't you, just for once, exhume your manners and be nice to him?
Sammy Nice?
Wilf It oughta be a woman. Nice always sounds better coming from a woman.

Suddenly, light dawns! Sammy is energized!

Sammy Yes! It's so simple it's brilliant! He's a straitlaced Englishman right? Well the close attentions of the right woman can leave your average straitlaced Englishman belly side up gasping for air!
Olive That isn't quite what I meant by "nice".
Sammy She doesn't have to do anything indecent, like marry him or anything. Just flirt a bit, gaze into his eyes, pretend he's interesting, blow in his ear. All we need is someone charming, warm, beautiful and sexy with enormous — acting abilities ...

Act I

Olive, taking this as a compliment, waits to be asked

Wilf, tell Amy I've got a job for her.

Wilf exits

Olive is hurt and offended. She goes to exit. Sammy is mystified

Olive I'm going.
Sammy Where?
Olive Out!
Sammy Olive … ?

Olive exits as Amy enters. Jeeps shoots on casually after Amy, obviously following her

Ah Amy, there you are.

Wilf comes back on

Jeeps. Find Strong and tell him wardrobe's ready, thank you.
Jeeps Now?
Sammy I wouldn't leave it that long.

Jeeps exits reluctantly

Sammy sighs

Amy What is it Sammy?
Sammy The show's in serious trouble, Amy.
Amy Oh no, can I help?
Sammy No, no, bless you. I couldn't ask you to …
Amy What?
Sammy It'll be all right won't it, Wilf?
Wilf (*unconvincingly*) Oh yes.
Amy Let me help. If something's wrong, then … Well, we're all in this together. It's up to all of us to do our bit …
Sammy Right — what you have to do is …

He whispers in her ear. She leaps up

Amy What! Oh no I couldn't!
Sammy You said we all have to give our bit.
Amy That was before I realized what bit you were asking me to give.

Sammy I'm only asking you to flirt — not spend your coupons on him.
Amy It wouldn't work. I can't flirt.
Sammy You? *You* can't flirt? Right. And Adolf Hitler's got a bit of a temper on him.
Wilf Amy — if you can't flirt why are half the blokes in this company in love with you?
Amy Don't be silly! They're not! Are they ——

Jeeps enters

— Jeeps?
Jeeps (*in agony*) I — I, well — I — I — Um — um ——
Amy See? Jeeps agrees — I can't flirt.

Jeeps' chance has gone. He could kick himself

Sammy OK. Fine — Don't worry.
Amy Really?

Olive comes crosses backstage, holding her fur coat

Sammy Olive — Olive love, don't go.
Olive I told you, I'm going out.
Sammy Please Olive, just a quick word, please …

He gives her a cup of tea. They sit down together

Olive All right. What?
Sammy Thank you. (*Sincerely*) Olive — I just wanted to say "sorry" that's all.
Olive (*genuinely touched*) What?
Sammy I've … well I've been a bit of a pig these last few weeks and I just wanted to apologize.
Olive Sammy …
Sammy You're far too good for me Ol, always have been.

He takes her hand and gazes into her eyes

> After all these years, and all you've had to put up with, you still manage to be warm, kind, sensitive, beautiful, intelligent, and I — I don't know what I'd do without you …

Olive (*sincerely touched*) Sammy, you and me, we've been ——

Sammy cuts across, to Wilf and Amy

Act I

Sammy Did you get that Amy? Did you get that? See it's simple... (*He drops Olive's hand and crosses to them*) Eye contact and flattery, eye contact and flat ——

Olive screams in frustration and exits, leaving her coat behind

Wilf (*with irony*) Well done Sammy.
Sammy It was nothing.

Wilf and Sammy lead Amy off, still coaching her

And laugh at his jokes.
Amy All right. (*A beat*) His what?

They're gone

Olive comes back to get her coat. Seeing the stage empty she sits at the piano and picks out a few notes. She sings the first few lines mournfully.

Olive (*singing*)   Just one more before we say good-night
Before we say good-night, one more

Gary enters at the back

Gary (*singing*)   Just one more before we fade away
To end a perfect day, one more.

Olive Gary! You remember!
Gary It was bread and butter for eighteen months, how could I forget? But you make it sound so sad. It wasn't like that, it was ...

He sweeps her up as a music hall back cloth comes in. A playbill from the Hartlepool Palladium with "Johnson and James" on the billing

Audience noise effect

The Lights change to music-hall style. A spot falls on Gary as he imitates a barker

Ladies and Gentlemen! Tonight, the Hartlepool Palladium is proud to present one of the foremost available acts — sorry, one of the four most available acts in the country — the couple who did for musical theatre — your own, your very own, Johnson and James!

Audience applause effect

Olive laughs and they slip into character and act out the song, both loving it

No. 6: Just One More

Gary   Just one more before we say good-night
Before we say good-night, one more
Just one more before we fade away
To end a perfect day, one more.

Olive   One more dance my dear
Very soon I shan't be here
Just one more before we say good-night
Let's make it just one more.

Gary   Can't you hear the music?
Can't you take a chance?
Put your arms around me
Let's dance …

I never cared for dancing
Till you came along
Olive   Everyone I danced with seemed wrong.

Both   Just one more before we say good-night
Before we say good-night, one more.

With music still held under the audience effect, they dance, every now and again stopping to exchange the banter

Gary Can you do the *paso doble*?
Olive Yes, but since the war broke out, I have to use powdered eggs.

They resume dancing

Oh don't you wish this night could last an eternity?
Gary Not really. My last bus leaves at nine.

More dancing

Do you believe that people dance the same way they make love?

Olive I hope not.
Gary Why?
Olive You just stopped before the music ended.

Gary
    I just live for dancing
    Dance the whole night through
    I'd go on for ever with you.

Showbiz — Gene Kelly street scene

Gary
    One more dance my dear
    'Cause very soon I shan't be here
Both
    Just one more before we say good-night
    Let's make it just one more.

Applause effect

They do showtime bows, and laugh — the backcloth is removed. The dream is over

Gary It was a good act ...
Olive While it lasted.

They pull apart. A moment

  You never wrote.
Gary Neither did you.
Olive I had nowhere to write to. You went to New York for a month and never came back.
Gary I'm sorry I'd planned on being an overnight success, then sending for you in triumph.
Olive It was a bloody long night.
Gary (*sighing*) I did miss you. I still do.

He puts his arm around her. She backs off

  Olive — you know the magic's still there.
Olive The magic may be, but after ten years you've got no right to wave your wand at me! I have a life now — I have — I mean, I'm ...
Gary (*getting it*) Sammy! Of course. Is it serious?
Olive You've met Sammy. How could I tell?
Gary With me you could always tell.

Gary takes her hand as Wilf enters holding the script

Wilf Er — hello. I hope I'm interrupting something.

They break

    Mr Strong, Sammy's waiting for you in the green room.
Gary I was just on my way. (*To Olive*) I'll see you later. (*He signs Wilf's script*) There you go.
Wilf Thank you.

Gary exits

(*Waving the autograph*) Is this worth money?
Olive On the basis that those things which are scarce are valuable — no.
Wilf (*tossing the script away*) You two seemed to be getting on well.
Olive We were just running through an old number, that's all.
Wilf It's funny. Some people have grandchildren, others have photographs. You and me, we measure out our lives in old numbers.(*A beat, then serious*) Look, Olive ...
Olive What?

Wilf backs off. He scribbles a note

Wilf As long as you're passing stage door, you couldn't do me a favour. Phone Alan and tell him a car's on its way to this address? (*He hands her the note*) Ta.

Olive reads the note

Olive Wilf? Your spelling is atrocious. Or to put it in language you'd understand – "atriocus". Didn't they do English at your school?
Wilf Not the morning I went.

Olive and Wilf exit. Bultitude comes on

Bultitude Mr Shaw? Mr Shaw?

Amy enters

Miss Chapman, have you seen Mr Shaw?

As Bultitude turns to get a chair, Sammy appears and pushes her closer

Amy No! *No* — No.

Act I

Bultitude What are you doing here?
Amy I — I ... (*Panicking*) I don't know ...

She sees Sammy US, *miming tea drinking*

Why a man of your stature hasn't been brought a cup of tea!

She goes US *to get one*

Sammy appears indicating to her that she should smile

Bultitude I say! Thank you.

She pulls up a chair next to him and adopts the same pose Gary pulled on her

Amy So Mr Bultitude, tell me all about yourself?
Bultitude Why?

This throws Amy

Amy Er— can you repeat the question?
Bultitude Why on earth would a young lady like yourself want to know anything about me?
Amy I'm interested! For instance, what made you want to be a producer?
Bultitude I didn't want to be a producer. I took the job after I was turned down.
Amy By whom?
Bultitude (*deadpan*) Everybody.

Sammy appears in the wings, egging her on

Amy Still. I bet it's demanding Mister B ...
Bultitude Bultitude. Heathcliffe Bultitude.
Amy What a divine name! It makes me think of passion and romance ...
Bultitude What? Bultitude?
Amy No, (*breathy*) Heathcliffe. Would you do what he did? Sacrifice all you had for the sake of a woman's love?
Bultitude No.
Amy Why not?
Bultitude My wife wouldn't like it. She doesn't like me out late.
Amy Well I hope that won't stop you coming to the party after the show?

He leaps up, outraged

Bultitude You have parties on BBC property? Oh no! I know all about showbusiness parties, with their drunkenness, filthy language, and lewd behaviour!

Amy But once the musicians have gone ...

Bultitude I'm sorry, but open a bottle of dandelion and burdock, put on a paper hat and, well — that's what sunk the Romans, you know!

Amy Why don't you like parties, the laughter, the music?

Bultitude Music! That isn't music. I studied music you know. The conservatory.

Amy The Paris Conservatory?

Bultitude No. My parents' conservatory.

Amy But we must have a party after such an important show.

Bultitude *No.* It is against regulations and they are embarrassing to me personally.

Amy Embarrassing?

Bultitude (*into the song*) It makes me remember ...

No. 7: I Took My Harp to a Party

Amy What do they make you remember?

Bultitude
They make me remember
A Christmas gone by
When I was extremely upset
A night in December
An evening that
I would very much rather forget.

I took my harp to a party
But nobody asked me to play
The others were jolly and hearty
But I wasn't feeling so gay.

They might have said
"Play us a tune we can sing."
But somehow I don't think they
Noticed the thing
I took my harp to a party
But nobody asked me to play
So I took the darned thing away.

They asked Mrs Morgan
To play her mouth organ
And somebody else did a dance

They let Mrs Carter
Perform a sonata
But I wasn't given a chance.

A north country person
Called Sandy McPherson
Played bagpipes and took off his coat
While both the Miss Fawcetts
Burst out of their corsets
In trying to take a top note.

I took my harp to a party
But nobody asked me to play
The others were jolly and hearty
But I wasn't feeling so gay.

I felt so ashamed at not striking a note
That I tried to hide the thing under my coat
I took my harp to a party
But nobody asked me to play
So I took the darned thing away.

Bultitude and Amy exit

The Lights fade to Black-out. Sammy, Wilf and Jeeps enter

The Lights come up on Sammy and Wilf trying to teach Jeeps how to do the ventriloquist act. He looks uncomfortable and is awful

Jeeps So tell me Nigel — where have you been this week? (*As the dummy*) G'ive geen to Gilly the Gaker in Garnstaple ... (*He gives up. To the others*) Couldn't he go to Harry the Hatmaker in Harrow?
Sammy Hopeless! We've got the first vent act in history with two dummies.
Wilf Come on Jeeps! You can do it!

Sammy pours a glass of water

Sammy (*handing Jeeps the glass*) Try again. Go on.

Jeeps takes the glass — reluctantly

Jeeps Ladies and gentlemen, I shall now attempt to sing *God Save The King* while Nigel drinks this glass of water.

Sammy Other way around ...
Jeeps (*with heavy heart*) Are you sure?

Sammy and Wilf nod

> OK. (*To the audience*) Other way around. Ahem! (*He starts drinking*) "God save our gracious Kig, log lig our nogle-*ahk*! *Rghhhkk*!

He starts choking. Sammy leaps into action

Sammy Oh my God — Nigel's drowning!

Jeeps keeps coughing and spluttering — water everywhere. Meanwhile, Sammy grabs the dummy and starts giving it the kiss of life, performing CPR etc. ...

> (*Mock tragic*) It's no good, I — I've lost him. (*He stands up and sighs*) Where the hell is Patterson?

Olive enters

Wilf Any news?
Olive Alan says the streets are so clogged no-one can get through.
Sammy Jeeps. You win. You're a sound man. And a damn fine one. Which is just as well ...

Sammy hands Jeeps some paper

Jeeps What's this?
Sammy The new opening. Rewrite. Final draft.
Jeeps (*scanning the pages*) Oh no! You've changed it! It's not set on a farm!
Sammy Will that be a problem?
Jeeps Yes! The sound effects, I'll never get them ready! I was relying on my coconuts!
Sammy A classic mistake amongst younger men.

Jeeps rushes off to his sound effects desk in a tizz, passing——

> *Amy, who enters with Bultitude. She nudges him towards the desolate crowd*

Amy They won't bite.
Bultitude Mr Shaw. In light of new evidence presented to me by Miss Chapman, you may keep the chicken song.

Act I

Amy And the French maid.
Bultitude Subject to the alteration.
Amy Isn't that wonderful?
Bultitude May I make that call now?
Amy Of course dear. Jeeps, the prompt corner phone please. I don't know what you were worried about, he's such a darling, once you get to know him. What's up Sammy, I thought you'd be pleased?
Sammy What? Sorry Amy, well done and all that, it's just ...
Wilf Alan can't make it.
Amy Oh no!
Sammy Unless I can find a replacement in the next ten minutes, we'll have to call the whole show off!

Bultitude is on the phone which is on the sound effects table

Bultitude It's me.... Yes I know I should have reported in earlier.... I know I promised him a bedtime story.... I know, I know, I know.... Not now. ... No, no, no.... All right, yes. Put him on. (*Voice change*) Hello Master Bultitude, this is your father. Would you like a bedtime story? ... Very well. Here is the story of the *Three Little Pigs*, whose ambition was to avoid being consumed by a wolf. So they each built a dwelling to protect them. The lazy pig built a house of straw, the less lazy one a house of wood and the clever, conscientious one, who I like to think of as Bultitude Pig, built a house of brick.

So the wolf arrived at the straw house and said:... (*wolf voice*) "Little pig, little pig — let me come in!" ... or words to that effect. And the pig replied: (*piggy voice*) "Not by the hair on my chinny chin chin." So the wolf said: (*wolf voice*) "I'll huff and I'll puff and I'll blow your house in!" And he did, and the lazy pig ran to his brother's wooden house: (*piggy voice*) "Help! Help! Save my bacon!" Then the wolf arrived (*wolf voice*): "Little pigs, little pigs — let me come in!" and lazy's brother said (*second pig voice*): "We'd rather not, if it's all the same to you, you furry rotter." I'm paraphrasing. So the wolf said: (*wolf voice*) "Right, mate, you asked for it!" and WHOOSHHH! Blew the house in!

So the two pigs took shelter in their brother's brick house. (*Wolf voice*) "Little pigs, little pigs — let me come in!" (*Third pig voice*) "Not by the hair on our chinny, chin, chin!" (*Wolf voice*) "I said LET ME IN! OR ELSE!" (*Third pig voice*) "Or else what, furface?" (*Wolf voice*) "I'll huff and I'll puff and I'll blow your house in!" And he ... (*he huffs*) and he (*he puffs*) ... and he (*he huffs*) and he (*he puffs*) ... and he (*he huffs*) and (*he puffs*) ... and he died of a haemhorrage caused by hyperventilation. So the moral is — always observe local building regulations or you'll be savaged by a wild animal. Tomorrow I'll tell you about *Rapunzel* and the value of personal grooming. But for now Master Bultitude; good-night! Nighty night night! Nightie nibbley-noo night!

He turns to find they're all looking at him

What? What is it?

They go into a huddle. Stop, turn and look at Bultitude, and resume the huddle again. They break and Sammy approaches

Sammy Mr Bultitude. "Bulty", "Bul", "B", could I have a quick word with you, man to man, professional to professional ...
Wilf Spider to fly.
Sammy I promise you, you won't regret this ...
Bultitude (*not realizing*) Regret what?

They lead him off

The Lights fade to Black-out

The tabs are closed. The rehearsal material is cleared. It's show time! The green light is turned on. Jeeps sorts out his sound effects (front of tabs)

The Band vamps awaiting Wilf

Wilf enters front of theatre, in costume for the show

No. 8: Hello to the Sun

Wilf Why do people all over the earth
Lie abed snoring for all they are worth
When they might be getting some fun
If they do as I do
Get up with the sun.

I'm up with the lark
As soon as it's day
I tear off the bedclothes
And throw them away
Before the day has really begun
I'm happy to say
Hello to the sun.

Act I

Wilf Good-evening ladies and gentlemen, my name's Wilfred Davies.

Honk from Jeeps on sound effects table

Thank you Mother, and welcome to the show. We've got some fabulous things lined up tonight as we broadcast live to the United States! We've got girls, gags, booze and loads of fun. But first we've got to get through the show. So let's start by bringing on a lady of many parts, most of them functional as well as decorative — the extraordinary Olive James!

Olive enters in a glamorous frock, as—

Jeeps holds up "Applause" sign. She and Wilf slip into an "I-say-I-say" double act

Olive Good-evening Wilfred. Any parties in tonight?
Wilf I understand we have a party in from Croydon.
Olive You don't say! My brother is working in Croydon this evening.
Wilf Really? What does he do?
Olive He's a burglar.

Drum crash

>   Though I seldom drink more than I ought
>   If any gentleman offers me port
>   There's a different story to tell
>   Though I rise quite early
>   I'm not very well.

Olive/Wilf
>   I'm up with the lark
>   I've not slept a wink
>   I tear off my nightie
>   And splash in the sink
>   The landlady's daughter
>   Is out for a run.
Olive
>   So I have to say
>   Hello to the sun.

Wilf Now ladies and gentlemen, you may notice those long things dangling above your heads — stop grinning, madam, they're only microphones. Microphones pick up *laughs*. So, if you hear anything funny — *laugh*. If you hear anything that might be funny — *laugh*. If you hear anything that's not funny — *laugh* anyway. And if you don't hear anything — you're deaf, what the *hell* are you doing at a radio show?

Everyone — turn round and shake hands with the person behind — I said *hands* madam — give a big grin to the person on your right and lend a fiver to the person on your left. See? We may not be funny, but at least we widen your circle of friends. In return, all we want is your unbridled hilarity. So come on, show us your teeth. I said show them madam, don't pass them round. And spare some applause too when I introduce you to the most beautiful broadside the Navy's ever seen — the Radio Girl Friend — Miss Amy Chapman.

Amy enters. Jeeps holds up "Applause" sign, and personally eggs the audience on, giving Wilf the thumbs up

Amy   I skip down the lane
                  I roll in the hay
                  I gather me rosebuds
                  And throw them away.

All   I sip the dew
                  It's excellent fun
                  While trying to say
                  Hello to the sun.

Jeeps Three minutes thirty Wilf.
Wilf Ladies and gentlemen, I want a special Variety Bandwagon welcome, as I bring on a member of the cast making his very first appearance on the show. New to this stage, but old everywhere else, ladies and gentlemen, the sophisticated, the debonair, Mr Jimmy Cut Glass Diamond!

Jeeps holds up the "Applause" sign as——

Bultitude is pushed on from the wings and stops like a rabbit caught in headlights. Wilf drags him CS

Jimmy, I hear your career is really taking off!
Bultitude Yes — it's er — er going very well in fact it's getting bigger all the time.
Wilf Well, watch out Jimmy. As Adam said to Eve in the garden of Eden: "Stand back Eve I don't know how big this thing is going to get."

Bultitude reacts, but it's time for his verse

Bultitude   It's too, too, good to be true
                  To do as I feel, and feel as I do.

Act I

All
We're up with the lark
We're happy that way
We're out and about
And happy to say
We're friends of all
And jealous of none
Just happy to say
Hello to the sun.

Jeeps Two minutes Wilf!
Wilf And now ladies and gentlemen, last and definitely least, I'd like to introduce the funniest and most popular man in the country — but sadly he's not available. So instead meet Variety Bandwagon's very own ray of sunstroke, the one and only Sammy "I'm-Doing-It" Shaw!

Jeeps cues applause. Sammy playfully cuffs Wilf

Sammy I'm-doing-it, I'm-doing-it!
(*Singing*) So heigh ho
I'm walking on air
With time on my hands
And straw in my hair.

All
I'm up with the lark
I'm out in the blue
I'm gone with the wind
I'm down with the flu
My day is done, before it's begun
I'm trying to say
Hello to the sun.

I'm up with the lark
I'm out in the blue
I'm gone with the wind
I'm down with the flu
My day is done, before it's begun
I'm trying to say
Olive Hello
Amy Hello
Bultitude Hello
Sammy/Wilf Hello
All Hello to the sun.

Jeeps cues applause

Jeeps Thirty seconds!
Sammy Thank you Wilf. That was Wilfred Davies, ladies and gentlemen — living proof of what happens when cousins marry. Good-evening everyone, it's good to see so many of you here. Is it raining out?
Wilf No boss — they've all come for a good laugh. They're really excited to see you.
Sammy (*peering at the audience*) So I see. If they were any more excited, they'd be awake.
Wilf And we've got a party from Croydon in.
Sammy I'll speak slowly then. Only kidding, m'luv.
Jeeps Fifteen seconds.
Sammy Fifteen seconds? What can we do in fifteen seconds?
Wilf We could tell some jokes!
Sammy You mean like — what do you get if you cross a leopard with a detective? Spotted dick!
Wilf Yes. Or — how do hedgehogs make love? Veeeery carefully!
Sammy Or — what's the difference between sex and an air raid? After an air raid, you don't have to visit a GP for the all clear. And here's another one you won't like ...
Jeeps Five seconds.
Sammy Oooops! Quippus interruptus! All right everybody — stand by your funny bones ... !

The CURTAIN *rises on the magnificent bandstand. The cast, (including the Grosvenors) take their places round the microphones as the band strikes up. The green light goes off as the red light and "On Air" sign go on*

No. 9: Let the People Sing

Grosvenors   Let the people sing
                   Let the people sing.

Bultitude (*as announcer, with microphone*) Good-evening. This is the BBC Light Programme being broadcast for the first time on the short wave to America. So settle down at home and abroad as Mr Sammy Shaw, star of stage, screen and London Underground invites you to to partake in another healthy portion of Variety Bandwagon.

All   Let the people sing
(*except Bultitude*) Sing like anything
                   Any sort of song they choose
                   Let the people sing
                   Let the welkin ring.

Act I   37

Principals (*except Bultitude*)	**Grosvenors**
Anything to kill the blues	To kill the blues
Find a merry song to cheer them	Ah
Tell them that I long to hear them.	Ah, to hear them.

All   When things all go wrong
You will find a song
Welcome as a breath of spring
Therefore let the people sing!

Jeeps cues applause

Sammy Sammy Shaw here. Good-evening ladies and gentlemen, here in the theatre in London and out there in radio land. This is Variety Bandwagon and you're welcome to it. Hello Wilf. Do we have a good show lined up for this evening?
Wilf Well, it's certainly a very fit show this week — 'cos we've all been evacuated to the Hope Springs Health Spa ——

Jeeps makes countryside noises, chickens, cows, sheeps at his table

(*With a helpless look; to Jeeps*) — a particular favourite with overweight barnyard animals. We are here to improve our bodies.

Jeeps covers his face with his coconuts (a neat trick if you can manage it)

Sammy And our brains Wilf.
Wilf I'm afraid I gave up on mine a long time ago.
Sammy Gave up?
Wilf Trying to find it.
Sammy But here at the Hope Springs Health Spa, set in the beautiful English countryside where we can hear typically English scenes. Like the sound of willow on leather.

Jeeps — Thwack effect

Wilf *Yarooo*!
Sammy But enough of Wilf's personal life. And, where you'll learn about that most British of all rituals ——

Olive enters with Simon, who's wearing a busby and red military tunic. They go up to Bultitude

Olive Mr Shopkeeper — I got this soldier for Christmas but I'd like to swap him for a pair of slippers.
Sammy — The Changing of the Guard. But first — let's check into the health spa. Open the door, Wilf ...

Jeeps — Creeakk effect!

Bultitude comes on as the manager

Bultitude (*as the manager*) Ah, Mr Shaw — I'm Mortimer Stodge, owner and proprietor of Hope Springs.
Sammy Not exactly an advert for the place, are you? I haven't seen that many chins since I looked in the Chinese phone directory.
Bultitude Well, really! I'll have you know, I've got the body of a man half my age.
Sammy Yes. And he's going to want it back later. I've got an appointment with the masseuse at two and I don't want to rub her up the wrong way. Where can I find her?
Bultitude Oh just follow the sound, sir.
Sammy What sound?

Jeeps — Screaming/slapping effects

Bultitude That sound.
Wilf Boss, that sounds like someone enduring the most agonizing torture imaginable!
Sammy Or possibly Gracie Fields tuning up.

Jeeps — Louder screaming/slapping effects!

All right Wilf. One of us has to go and pick our star guest up from the station and one of us has to go in for a massage.

Jeeps — Footsteps on gravel tray — receding effect

Wilf (*a long way away*) See you when I get back from the station.
Sammy Well — here goes ...

Jeeps — knock knock. Door opening effects

Bultitude (*with a Swedish accent*) Ooooh hullo, Mister Shaw.
Sammy Oh no, it's Helga Steelvelda — the Hard Boiled Swede!
Bultitude (*as Helga*) Ya. You are coming for your two o'clock massacre?

Act I

Sammy I think you mean "massage"?
Bultitude See if you still do at three o'clock. Please be taking off your clothes.
Sammy All of them?
Bultitude Mr Shaw, I am a professional. Nudity doesn't scare me.
Sammy No full length mirrors in your house, obviously. All right — I'll take them off but I trust we won't be interrupted!

Jeeps — Door opening effect

Bultitude switches accents — to being the Colonel

Bultitude (*as Colonel*) I say! Is this the way to the bar?
Sammy Colonel Quixsnort! No. No, it isn't but if you find it — mine's a large one.
Bultitude Really. Must be a trick of the light. Well, toodle-pip.

Jeeps — Door shutting effect

Sammy He went to Oxford you know. Should have stayed the night!

Jeeps — Cracking effect

  Ooooh! Helga — do you have to do that?
Bultitude (*as Helga*) You object to me cracking my knuckles?
Sammy When you do it with a mallet — yes.
Bultitude Just lay on the table and we'll begin ...

Jeeps — Slapping effect

Sammy G-g-good Lord — please be careful — I'm rather attached to my body.

Jeeps — Boing effect

  — and I'll thank you to leave that alone.

Jeeps — Boing effect. Sound of door opening

Olive (*as Lou Lou, the French maid*) Mr Shaw — would you like me to polish your knick-knacks?
Sammy Well blow me! It's luscious Lou Lou, the French maid! Come to my room later and we'll plump some pillows together.

Olive Mister Shaw, you saucy man. No, no, no!
Sammy A-ha the French resistance!

Jeeps — Sound of door shutting. Slapping effect

    A-anyway, as I was saying, this woman came up to me and she said ...
Bultitude (*as Helga*) Are you always this stiff?
Sammy I beg your pardon?
Bultitude Your body — it is so tense! Are you knowing why? It is like a coiled spring.

Jeeps — Boing effect

Sammy ... and I won't tell you again. Don't touch that! Thank you Helga — that will be all.

We hear air raid sirens; (not from Jeeps' sound effects table)

Jeeps — Door opening effect

Wilf Boss, boss — I forgot to ask; who am I picking up? Who's our star guest?
Sammy Wilf, he's one of your Hollywood heroes!
Wilf Someone I've always wanted to be like?
Sammy Yes, yes.
Wilf Has he got brown hair, brown eyes and wonderful teeth?
Sammy Yes, yes, yes.
Wilf At last, Rin-Tin-Tin!
Sammy It's not Rin-Tin-Tin, Wilfred. It's ...
Wilf Errol Flynn?
Sammy Don't be silly Wilfred. What would Errol Flynn be doing in a war zone? No it's ...

Sammy whispers to Wilf

Wilf Boss, I'm gone.

Jeeps — Whizz siren effect

Sammy Who was that gas masked man?

Jeeps — Whizz siren effect

    You're back!

Act I   41

Wilf And look who I've brought ...

Jeeps — Door opening effect

Gary Hello everybody!
Sammy Why if it isn't that international star of stage and screen, Mr Gary Strong!

Jeeps holds up the "Applause" card. Door opening effect

Olive (*as Lou Lou*) Mr Shaw, you naughty boy, you 'aven't introduced me to your luvvverly, 'andsome new friend! Tell me, does 'e need any cleaning done? I can't wait to run my duster over 'is ornaments!
Gary Pleased to meet you, ma'am. I'm Gary — no, Pilot Officer Strong, RAF — I'd do anything to further international affairs.

Olive and Gary are genuinely flirting

Olive (*as Lou Lou*) Oh — so would I! You know they say French is the language of love — well, I could teach you 'ow to *kiss* in French!
Gary That really is very kind of you.
Olive Not at all. After all, you know what they say about we French. We only 'ave a tiny resistance! Do you see my love birds over there? Snuggled up tightly as if they haven't a care in the world.

Jeeps — Tweet, tweet effect

Gary Yes.
Olive Would you like to do that?
Gary I'd love to, but I don't think we'd fit in the cage.
Olive In that case, 'ow about a little kiss?

Sammy forces his way between them to get to the microphone

Sammy Excuse me! No time, but it is time for a song, without further ado, boys in the band, on your laundry marks, get set, cue — Gary Strong!

No. 10: Oh Buddy I'm in Love

Gary   I'm dreamy all day
                 I'm awake half the night
                 I've liquidated a good appetite

You can't feel so gay
When you're feeling so flat
There's only one thing
That gets you like that.

It looks like love
It feels like love
I'm acting like a turtle dove
Oh Buddy I'm in love
Oh Buddy I'm in love.

Gary all too obviously sings toward Olive

I act so soft
I feel so strange
You must have seen
A great big change
Oh Buddy I'm in love
Oh Buddy I'm in love.

This morning I went to the doctor
To ask him what's wrong with me
He told me that I had love-i-tis
As badly as it could be.

Oh it looks like love
It feels like love
I'm cooing like a turtle dove
Oh Buddy I'm in love
Oh Buddy I'm in love.

This morning I went to the doctor
To ask him what's wrong with me
He told me that I had love-i-tis
As badly as it ever could be.

In the background the raid starts

Oh it looks like love
It feels like love
I'm cooing like a turtle dove
Oh Buddy I'm in love
Oh Buddy I'm in love
Oh Buddy I'm in love.

Act I   43

Jeeps cues applause

The raid's now fairly fierce — definitely audible to folks listening at home. Sammy has communicated to the band

Sammy Well b's and g's the storm clouds have gathered over Europe, and where we are it's chucking it down. But we do know who's responsible, and we know what to do …

He rallies everybody

No. 11: Who's Been Polishing the Sun

Sammy	This world's becoming a gay one I used to think it a grey one But I discovered it's "A"- one just now It's taken on a new meaning It's very nice to be seen in There's been a little spring cleaning somehow.
	Who's been polishing the sun? Brightening the sky today They must have known just how I like it Everything's coming my way.
Grosvenors	Who's been teaching all the birds How to sing a roundelay?
Sammy **Grosvenors**	They must have known just how I like it Everything's coming my way.
Sammy	Yesterday everything looked anyhow Then I met someone and look at it now.
Grosvenors **Sammy**	Who's been polishing the sun? Rubbing out the clouds of grey They must have known just how I like it Ev'rything's coming my way.
Sammy	Tell me who's been polishing the sun Sweeping all the stormy clouds away They must have known just how I like it Every little thing's gonna be OK.

| Grosvenors | Tell me who's been teaching all the birds |
| | How to sing a merry roundelay? |

Boys 1/Girls 3	Girls 2	Girls1/Boys 2
Fa la la la		
La la la la	Fa la la la	
La la la.	La la la.	Fa la la.

| Sammy | They must have known just how I like it |
| Grosvenors | Mmm. Everything's coming your way. |

Sammy	Yesterday everything looked anyhow
	Then I fell in love with the sweetest little girl
All	And look, look, look at it now.

Sammy	Who's
Grosvenors	Who's
Sammy	Been
Grosvenors	Been
Sammy ⎫	Polishing the sun?
Grosvenors ⎭	Rubbing out the nasty clouds of grey
Grosvenors	They must have known just how we like it.
Sammy	(*speaking*) OK boys — take it away.

Tap break

| All | Who's been polishing the sun? |
| | Rubbing out the clouds of grey |

Sammy		Grosvenors
They must have known		They must have known
Just how I like it.		How I like it.

Sammy	Everything
Grosvenors	Everything
Sammy	Everything
Grosvenors	Everything
All	Everything's coming my way!

Jeeps cues applause

Act I

No. 11A: Who's Been Polishing The Sun (Reprise)

Sammy begins the reprise a cappella

Sammy	Yesterday everything looked anyhow
(Band in)	Then I fell in love with the
	Sweetest little girl
All	And look, look, look at it now.

Who's been polishing the sun?
Rubbing out the clouds of grey.

Sammy	**Grosvenors**
They must have known	They must have known
Just how I like it.	How I like it.

Sammy	Everything
Grosvenors	Everything
Sammy	Everything
Grosvenors	Everything
All	Everything's coming my way!

BOOM! A massive explosion is heard, seemingly mere yards from the theatre, drowning out the reprise

Bultitude steps forward, as the cast prepares to leave the stage

Sammy waits until last, watching Gary lead Olive off

Bultitude Ladies and gentlemen. The management has decided you would be safer on the lower levels of the theatre. Transmission will continue as soon as the all-clear sounds. Thank you.

The tabs come in. Sammy is seen slowly leaving the stage as——

The Lights go to Black-out

ACT II

Scene 1

Entr'acte

The tabs rise to reveal the alcove by the stage door. Olive is discovered in the wings, seated alone. Outside the raid continues. A bomb drops close by and she shivers

No. 12: Someone Else

Olive   A quiet lunch, that is all that it is
It doesn't mean I'll change my name to his
And yet he's caring and kind
It's no wonder I find
That my head's in a sort of a tiz.

There's someone else in this world not just you
There's someone else doing things you don't do
He says words I like to hear
He's so nice to be near
Lunch may last for a decade or two.

I'm all at sea there is no doubt of that
Choose a man?
I couldn't choose a hat
Which way shall I go?
Real life is so unreal.

If this goes on love may lose its appeal
For if I make one mistake
One two three hearts may break
Someone please tell my heart what to feel.

Gary enters

Act II, Scene 1 47

Gary There you are. Shouldn't you be downstairs with the others?
Olive You mean dispensing warm tea and forced jollity like the English are supposed to do in times of crisis? No thanks. I need to smell the air.
Gary I know what you mean.

He lights two cigarettes and passes her one

Olive Thanks.

A bomb explodes near by. He jumps more than she does

This is all new to you isn't it?
Gary I'll say. Until last week the closest I'd ever come to a bomb was playing Iago to Victor Mature's Othello. The greatest threat to my existence was Hedda Hopper.
Olive Why did you come back? They couldn't have made you.
Gary I don't know. A sense of duty perhaps. The thought of missing out. Maybe I'd just seen too many movies. (*He takes her hand*) I'm glad I'm here.

Olive tries to change the subject

Olive When do you have to report in?
Gary Northfield aerodrome, Monday 0600. Which means we can meet tomorrow.

He moves closer. She gets up

Olive Gary.
Gary What?
Olive It's been ten years! You can't just waltz in here and pick me up like — like I'm some book you never finished! I'm not the same Olive James. I'm different. I have responsibilities.
Gary So do I.

He crosses to her

But who knows how long either will last. Look I can't make up for the past, and I can't promise anything for the future. All any of us have is now.

He kisses her on the back of the neck, then goes to exit to the surface

Remember, we were a great team.

Olive Where are you going?
Gary Up top. You need time to think. And I want to see what I've got myself into.

Gary exits

Olive re-lights her cigarette

Wilf enters

Wilf Oy! Put that light out!
Olive Wilf! It's only you.
Wilf Story of my life!

A bomb goes off in the distance. He jumps

Olive That was miles away Wilf, there's no need to be frightened.
Wilf Maybe not. But when there is a need, I'll be ready.

He peers out of the exit

Trying out another old number were you? How did it go? Sammy's looking for you.
Olive I'll be right down.
Wilf He needs you, you know.
Olive I need me too.
Wilf Coming?
Olive In a minute.

He waits

I said in a minute.

Wilf exits

No. 12A: Someone Else (Reprise)

Olive I'm all at sea there is no doubt of that
Choose a man?
I couldn't choose a hat!
Which way shall I go?
Real life is so unreal

Act II, Scene 2

> If this goes on love may lose its appeal
> For if I make one mistake
> One two three hearts may break
> Someone please tell my heart what to feel.
>
> A gentleman who never treats you rough
> Sounds just fine
> But is it quite enough?
>
> Someone else may know all the right things to say
> And he may know all the right moves to play
> But then could I ever get the same thrill that I get
> When your face faces my way
> I may find out some day.

Scene 2

In front of the tabs, in the wings of the radio stage. Sammy is asleep, slumped against the prop table

Wilf enters and goes up behind him. He does a quick tap dance

Wilf (*loudly*) Five minutes, Mr Shaw!
Sammy (*waking*) I'm-doing-it! I'm-doing-it!

He sees it's Wilf and groans

    Wilf. I must have dropped off.
Wilf I don't know, you young comedians. You work eighteen hours a day and all you can think about is sleep!

Wilf gets out a flask and swigs

Sammy I'm shattered. I can't carry on like this, I'll end up looking like you. Where's Olive? And what's that?
Wilf Brandy.

Sammy takes a nip

Sammy It's real too. Where d'you get it?
Wilf D'you remember Marty Stevens? Had that cat and mouse act — Blacky and Snowy?
Sammy "Nature's Enemies But The Best Of Friends". Yeah. What of him?

Wilf He's the new barman at the *Savoy*. The mouse died in Leeds.
Sammy Oh we've all died in Leeds, dear. You didn't answer my question — where's Olive?
Wilf She said she'll be right down.
Sammy Was she alone? (*A pause*) I thought so.
Wilf Look Sammy ...
Sammy You don't have to "look Sammy" me Wilf, I know what's going on.
Wilf You do?
Sammy Of course I do! I'm pig-headed and insensitive, I'm not blind. How could she do this to me?
Wilf Sammy. Trust me. I'm used to your abuse. Your neglect, your thoughtlessness, your greedy, selfish, inconsiderate, tactless, insensitive behaviour ...
Sammy Hey! What about my good qualities?
Wilf Those *are* your good qualities. Olive needs more. Deserves more. And what she wants from you, she's getting from him.
Sammy If all she wants are kind words and a pretty face, she can have him!
Wilf Just tell her.
Sammy What? That she's free to go?
Wilf That you love her. That you need her. And that you're sorry.
Sammy God, I'm so tired.

Jeeps enters as the all-clear sounds

Sammy returns to type

Jeeps Sammy, we've got the all-clear.
Sammy Well done Jeeps, award yourself a coconut! As if you needed another.

Gary enters

Gary, there you are. Ready for the second half?
Gary I hope so.
Sammy Then damn the torpedoes, let's give them a night to remember eh?

With his arm around Gary he leads him off. Wilf tugs at him from behind

Wilf What are you going to do about ...
Sammy I'm-doing-it, I'm-doing-it.

They exit

Act II, Scene 3

SCENE 3

Scene change to radio show. The CURTAINS *open. The green light goes off. The red light and "On Air" sign go on*

Bultitude Ladies and gentlemen, welcome back to this very special transatlantic Variety Bandwagon broadcast, being brought to you from the very depths of the Blitz in the glittering heart of London's West End, the cradle of the glorious British Empire and Commonwealth, on which the sun never sets and in which, to quote Kipling ...
Sammy Let's get on with it!
Bultitude Really! Have you no respect for Kipling?
Sammy I don't know, I've never Kippled. Let's turn on the music ladies and gentlemen. In a military manner with Amy Chapman, the Grosvenors and Miss Olive James!

The medley involves all the Grosvenors with Amy and Olive sharing lead on "The King's Horses", the Grosvenors taking "The Fleet's in Port" and Olive leading, (though backed by Amy) on "A Girl Who Loves a Soldier"

No. 13: Military Medley

The King's Horses

Olive }	The King's horses
Amy	The King's men
Amy	March down the street
Olive	And then march back again
Amy/Olive }	The King's horses,
Grosvenors	And the King's men.
Olive }	They're in scarlet
Amy	They're in gold
Olive	All dollied up
Amy	It's a joy to behold.
Amy/Olive }	The King's horses
Grosvenors	And the King's men
Amy	They're not out to fight the foe
	You might think so
Olive	But oh dear no
	They're out because they've got to go to put
	A little pep into the Lord Mayor's show.

Olive/Amy ⎫ **Grosvenors** ⎭	It's their duty now and then To march down the street And to march back again The King's horses And the King's men.

Segue

The Fleet's in Port

Grosvenors	The fleet's in port again Back home in port again Yo-ho, yo-ho, Now we'll have a jolly good time.
Girls	The boys are here to find The girls they left behind
Boys	Yo-ho, yo-ho
Grosvenors	Now we'll have a jolly good time.
Boys	Ladies turn out in your thousands Put on your red white and blue
Girls	All the nice girls love a sailor
Boys	There'll be a sailor for you.
Grosvenors	Because the fleet's in port again Back home in port again Yo-ho, yo-ho
Boys	Now we'll have a jolly good
Girls	Really wonderful
Grosvenors	Mighty marvellous time.

Segue

There's Something About a Soldier

Olive	There's something about a soldier
Amy	Something about a soldier
Olive/Amy ⎫ **Grosvenors** ⎭	Something about a soldier That is fine fine fine.
Olive	He may be a great big general
Amy	May be a sergeant major

Act II, Scene 3

Olive/Amy ⎫	May be a simple private
Grosvenors ⎭	Of the line line line.
Olive	But there's something
	About his bearing
Amy	Something in what he's wearing
Olive/Amy ⎫	Something about his buttons
Grosvenors ⎭	All a-shine shine shine
Olive	Oh! A military chest
	Seems to suit the ladies best
Olive/Amy ⎫	There's something about a soldier
Grosvenors ⎭	That is fine fine fine.

Tap break

Segue

A Girl Who Loves a Soldier

Olive ⎫	She simply can't refuse him
Amy ⎬	Oh! How she'd hate to lose him
Grosvenors ⎭	For the girl who weds a soldier
	Is the girl who adores a parade
	She becomes herself a soldier
	She's a part of the grand cavalcade!

Jeeps cues applause

Bultitude enters and steps up to the microphone

Bultitude Now it's time to welcome back your friend and mine, Mr Sammy Shaw!

Sammy enters

Sammy I'm doing-it! I'm doing-it! Yes, hello folks, we're back. Sorry about the break in transmission but someone forgot to put a shilling in the meter. Never mind — we're all still here, at the Hope Springs Health Spa and Bingo Hall, where it's dinner time. Nothing like a roast bird is there? Can't wait to get hold of that stuffing ...
Bultitude (*as Gobble-dee-Gook*) WHOOOOOH! Kindly warm your hands, sir.
Sammy Well, if it isn't Gobble-dee-Gook, the talking goose!

Bultitude Ee Mr Shaw, this ain't been a good day. Not since I started moulting. I woke up this morning with a beakful of me own feathers!
Sammy I thought you looked down in the mouth. Open wide, and let's have a gander.

Drum crash

Bultitude Aaaaaahhhhh!
Sammy Hmmm. Your giblets are enlarged. And not in a good way. I'd make a vet your next port of call ...

Jeeps — Door opening effect

Bultitude now plays the Colonel

Bultitude (*as the Colonel*) Did someone say "port"?
Sammy Not now Colonel. Colonel, have you met Mr Gobble-dee-Gook?

This is meant as a tease. Bultitude rises to it

Bultitude (*as Colonel*) Hello. (*As Gobble-dee-Gook*) Hello.
Sammy Now where's our announcer ... Never mind. Mr Gook, where are you going?
Bultitude To join the other geese, Mr Shaw. Surely you know about migrating?
Sammy Of course I know about migrating. It's what I keep under mifireplace.

Drum crash

And now ladies and gentlemen the Radio Magician will attempt a very difficult optical illusion, never before seen on the wireless. Mephisto!
Wilf (*as Mephisto; Eastern mystic*) Oh yes indeed — I am going to saw this lady in half.
Sammy This lady ... ?
Wilf No, this lady, in the box.
Sammy This is obviously a very dangerous trick ladies and gentlemen, so I am going to ask for complete silence.

Drum roll

I said silence, there's a man drumming.

Drum stops

Act II, Scene 4

Thank you. Mephisto!
Wilf Thank you Mr Shaw.

Jeeps — Saw noise. Boing. Eek. Noisy crash effects

Oh dear.
Sammy Never mind. Those were not new trousers! I hope not. Thank you Mephisto. The frontiers of wireless pushed ever backwards! Well, bless my dover sole if it isn't our reader of letters and words as well, the Radio Girl Friend, Miss Amy Chapman. Hello Amy, what are you doing here?
Amy Well, it's that time of the week again.
Sammy It is? Oh yes, so it is. Ladies and gentlemen, Miss Amy Chapman!

Jeeps holds up the "Applause" sign as we change scene to the wings

Amy (*during the wipe*) Hello everyone out there. But most of all hello to those of you who've taken the time to write to me over the past week or so ...

The scene change is almost complete

I can only read a few out on air, but I assure you I'll be answering all personal requests as soon as I can — My first letter comes from Mary Stevens who used to live ...

Scene 4

Sammy pulls Wilf off into the wings as Amy continues reading out letters and replies

Wilf What's wrong? What's wrong?
Sammy Nothing's wrong. I've had an idea. I want you to ...

He whispers in Wilf's ear. He pretends to be shocked

Wilf I think you should ask my parents first!
Sammy Stop it! This is serious. It's about Gary. Will you do it? For me?
Wilf All right. For you Sammy and no-one else.
Sammy You're a pal. Now are you sure you've got it?
Wilf I'll write it down.

They search themselves for paper

Paper ...

Sammy Ah! I've got some!

From his pocket he pulls out the green security clearance form. Both are horrified

Wilf Bloody hell! The security clearance! You said you'd done it! Sammy, you idiot!
Sammy I filled it in.
Wilf But you didn't hand it in! Do you know what this means?
Sammy It means nothing. Look, we're still on air aren't we? I'll bet they haven't even noticed ...
Wilf If Bultitude finds out, he'll cancel the show. Permanently!
Sammy True. But listen, I've had this fantastic idea.
Wilf What?
Sammy Let's not tell him.
Wilf Someone's coming. Hide it!

Sammy gives it to Wilf

Sammy You hide it!

Wilf gives it back

Wilf No, you hide it.

As they're squabbling, Bultitude enters from behind, he sees it

Bultitude (*letting out a cry of pure pain*) Aaaaaaaaaaaaagggggggggggghhhhhhhhhhh!
Wilf } (*together*) Shhhhhhhhhhhhhhhhhhhhhhhh!
Sammy }
Bultitude You told me you'd done it, you promised!
Wilf That's just what I said.
Bultitude I'm ruined, understand, ruined. Not only have I appeared in a light entertainment show under a false name, it wasn't even cleared! What'll I say? What can I say? They'll believe I wasn't involved. They'll think I'm incompetent, or worse, working for the enemy — I'll be sent to work in a munitions factory — or down the mines — or worse — ENSA! (*Final panic*) What will Eileen say!
Sammy Steady on Heathcliffe, you're panicking. Take a few deep breaths ... (*He turns to Wilf*) Haven't you got a little job to do?
Wilf Er, yes, of course.

Act II, Scene 4

Wilf exits

Bultitude You lied to me! — I've got to inform the authorities!

He lurches for the phone. Sammy pulls him back

Sammy You can't. The lines are down.
Bultitude Then we must stop the show. I must stop the show!
Sammy Stop the show? Now? Are you mad? Think of all the people up and down the country who'll be listening. Shell-shocked people, people tired and afraid. Some of them may have even lost their homes tonight. Well obviously they won't be listening, but think of the others. Do you want to be responsible for them losing the only thing they have left?
Bultitude What?
Sammy Us! Us! We may be their last ray of sunshine in a grey and hopeless world.
Bultitude Well, I don't ...
Sammy Think of them, Heathcliffe. Picture them in your mind. Old people, young people, some more old people, rich people, poor people — maybe — maybe even — the King! (*He salutes*)
Bultitude The King.
Sammy And if not him, think of the children.
Bultitude You mean Margaret Rose and Elizabeth?
Sammy No, not the — Yes! Yes, them too! Think of Margaret and Elizabeth and all the children up and down the country, dressed in rags with tear-stained faces, huddled round the wireless, praying for that ray of sunshine — can you see them, Heathcliffe?
Bultitude Well I ...
Sammy Of course you can! They're sad aren't they? But have they given up? Of course they haven't! Because somehow we're giving them the strength to carry on. And you're part of that strength, Heathcliffe. We've been bombed, blitzed, locked in a cellar but did you waver? Did you falter? Of course you didn't! Why Heathcliffe, you're not a man — you're — you're a rock! A brick! Yes. A total brick.

Sammy turns Bultitude round to face him

Face facts, Heathcliffe! Your country needs YOU!
Bultitude Mr Shaw — you're absolutely right!
Sammy I am?
Bultitude When I'm on stage and everyone's looking at me, I can feel a special warmth flowing through the audience. It's a good warmth isn't it?
Sammy The best.

Bultitude What we're doing here isn't just a collection of old jokes, bad puns and cheap characters ...

Sammy chokes

It's at the forefront of the battle for morale! Why — closing it down would be tantamount to ...
Sammy Aiding and abetting the enemy?
Bultitude Precisely! Do you know what I say to silly security clearances?
Sammy What?
Bultitude Biscuits!

Sammy swoons

We deserve medals from the King! The King!

They both salute, Sammy from prone

Sammy The King! (*He gets up*)
Bultitude We're not performers, we're heroes!
Sammy Rule Britannia.
Bultitude And you stand there worrying about bits of paper. Really Mr Shaw!
Sammy Sorry.
Bultitude Never mind. Have you got your script?

Sammy nods

Bultitude Good. We're on.

Wilf shoots on from the back

Have you done it?
Wilf Yes, what's happening?
Sammy The second half of course!

The scene changes and we go back to the closing moments of Amy's speech

Act II, Scene 5   59

                                    SCENE 5

Amy is CS

Amy Anyway listeners, that's all we've got time for this week. If you have any personal requests, remember to send them to me, Amy Chapman, your Radio Girl Friend at the usual address …

The change to full stage has been completed

Sammy Thank you, Amy Chapman.

Wilf enters with a prop telephone

Wilf Mr Shaw, Mr Shaw — Sammy — there's a telephone call for you.
Sammy Who is it, I'm busy?
Wilf It's a man from Wales.
Sammy Tell him I'll call him Bach.

Wilf exits

As I was saying ladies and gentlemen …

Wilf enters with the telephone

Wilf Mr Shaw. Telephone call. It's a man with one leg.
Sammy Well tell him to hop it!
Wilf It's a man with one leg called Smith.
Sammy Well ask him what the other one is called.

Wilf exits

Apologies for the interruption ladies and gentlemen. There comes a time in …

Wilf enters with the phone

Wilf Telephone for Mr Shaw. It's Marvel the tightrope walker.
Sammy Tell him to get off the line.

Wilf exits. Bultitude enters as the health spa manager

Bultitude (*as the manager*) Mr Shaw. Hark!

Sammy At my age?
Bultitude Mr Shaw — as manager of this health spa, I must tell you I take a very dim view ——
Sammy So it does effect your eyesight!
Bultitude A very dim view of your cavalier attitude to spa rules. I hear you've even had a woman in your room!
Sammy That's just Lou Lou. She comes in to provide my evening turn down service.
Bultitude Are you sure that's all?
Sammy Absolutely, I tell her how I want my bed warmed, and she turns me down.
Bultitude Outrageous! Whatever next?

Irene enters, crossing the stage

Irene Mr Shaw, Mr Shaw. I am so lonely, so sad and alone.
Sammy Whatever happened to your fiancé, my dear, I thought you were engaged?
Irene I was engaged to an eskimo.
Sammy Don't tell me, you broke it off!

Irene exits

What a girl, she was only an Alderman's daughter but she let the Borough surveyor.

Daisy enters

Daisy Is it time for the next number yet. Are you ready?
Sammy I'm-doing-it. I'm-doing-it. Don't rush me, I'm just talking to the boys and girls.
Daisy Well the band are getting restless Sammy, only just now the trumpet player suggested ... (*she whispers in Sammy's ear*)
Sammy But that's outrageous — off you go young lady and cool down.

Daisy exits

What a girl, boys and girls. She was only a policeman's daughter, but she never came quietly! It is indeed time for a musical interlude, so if you are into lewd music, this song is for you!

Intro to "Ali Baba"

Act II, Scene 5

Wilf Oh Gary, Bill at stage door asked me to give you these ...

Wilf hands Gary a bundle of letters, phone numbers etc. Gary starts autographing them

Gary (*holding out the phone numbers*) Want to take these?
Wilf I already have. Oh and there was this ...

Wilf hands Gary a telegram. He opens it. Instant effect

Gary Damn. I've got to go ...
Wilf Now? What about the next number?
Gary (*pulling off his costume*) Can't be helped I'm afraid. They want me to report to base immediately! Wilf, tell Olive I'll call her the first moment I get. And say goodbye to the others. Tell them I said thanks. Bye Wilf.

Gary shakes Wilf's hand and exits

The scene is set for the next number. This is really where Jeeps' sound effects come into their own (lots of Eastern bells, gongs, whistles, sand effects etc.)

No. 14: Ali Baba's Camel

Sammy	You've heard of Ali Baba Forty thieves had he Out for what we all want Lots of LSD.*
Wilf	He also had a camel Stole it from a zoo
Sammy **Wilf** }	How he loved the camel And the camel loved him too.
Band	Oh! Oh! Oh! Oh! Oh! How the camel loved Ali Baba!
Sammy **Wilf** } **Wilf**	Ali Baba's camel Loved Ali Baba so No matter where he went to The camel had to go
Sammy	Some say that he's in heaven But this I know is true

* *Librae, solidi, denarii* (pounds, shillings, and pence)

Wilf	Wherever you think Ali's gone,
Both	His camel's gone there too.

The Camel enters

Wilf	Crossing the equator
	It was as hot as this
Sammy	He was so very thirsty
	And everybody knows
	It's horrible to walk for miles
	With sand between your toes.
Band	Oh! Oh! Oh! Oh!
	Oh! How the camel loved Ali Baba!
Sammy ⎫	Ali Baba's camel
Wilf ⎭	Turned round and licked his hand
Sammy	He said:
Bultitude	Oh Ali Baba
(*off; as Camel*)	You surely understand
	We must find an oasis
	And get a drink somehow
	But hark I hear the temple bells
	They'll all be open now.
Band	La la la la la la
	La la la la la la
Wilf	He entered it for races
	At the desert sports
Sammy	There goes Ali's camel
	In 'is filthy cotton shorts.
Wilf	The starter cracks his/her pistol
	Off the camels tear
Sammy ⎫	Ali Baba's camel wins
Wilf ⎭	By half a camel's hair
Band	Oh! Oh! Oh! Oh!
	Oh! How the camel loved Ali Baba!
All	Ali Baba's camel
	Had run for miles and miles

Act II, Scene 5

Sammy	Its tail was pointing backwards
Wilf	(*spoken; Groucho Marx style*)
	That's how a camel smiles.
Sammy ⎫	But Ali and his camel
Wilf ⎭	They both were out of breath
Wilf	They'd run so far
Sammy	They'd laughed so much
Both	They'd laughed themselves to death.
Band	Ah ha-ha hee hee-hee!
All	Ali Baba's camel
	Loved Ali Baba so
	No matter where he went to
	The camel had to go.

		Grosvenors
Sammy ⎫	Some say that he's in heaven	Ooh
Wilf ⎭	But this I know as well	Ooh, Ah
	Wherever you think Ali's gone	
	His camel's gone to …	

Jeeps — Honk! effect

Jeeps cues applause. Close tabs. Play off music

Sammy (*front of tabs*) So much for Ali Baba. But what a polite camel. He asked me whether I wanted one hump or two!

Jeeps — Bang bang! effect (clappers)

Bultitude enters dressed up as Farmer Giles

Bultitude (*as Farmer Giles*) Which why did he go?
Sammy Oh no! It's old Giles from the farm next door!
Bultitude Sorry Mr Shaw. Did I be giving you a shock?
Sammy I'll say you did be. Don't point that horrible thing at me. And put your gun away while you're at it. Have you got a licence for that thing?
Bultitude No. Only for the gun …
Sammy What're you after?
Bultitude Oh a devil of a rabbit sir. He's been nibbling my prize plums.
Sammy Few of us are that lucky. But if you want to shoot on this land you'll need a licence. Normally it costs sixpence, but to you — five shillings.
Bultitude Can I pay with this?

Jeeps — Cluck cluck! effect

Sammy Sorry. I never accept personal chicks!

Drum crash

Bultitude Oh look sir! There he goes!

Jeeps — Boing boing! effect

Stop! Stop that Bunny!
Sammy Well fancy that! Old Farmer Giles chasing a rabbit with a gun. Bail me out of Bow Street if that baint the cue for a song!

Open tabs on the Grosvenors

No. 15: Run, Rabbit, Run

Boys 2	Run, rabbit,		
	Run, rabbit, run,		
Boys	Run, run, run,	**Girls**	(Run), run,
All	Run.		
Boys 1	Rabbit, run, rabbit, run		
Boys	Run, run, run,	**Girls**	(Run), run,
All	Run.		
B and G 2	Rabbit, run, rabbit,		
All	Run.		
B and G 1	Rabbit, run, rabbit,		
All	Run.		
B and G 2	Rabbit		
All	Run.		
B and G 1	Rabbit,		
All	Run.		
B and G 2	Rabbit,		
All	Run.		
B and G 1	Rabbit		
All	Run, rabbit, run, rabbit,		
	Run, rabbit, run, rabbit,		
	Run, run, run, run, run.		

Act II, Scene 5

                On the farm, every Friday
                On the farm, (*Ohh aar*) it's rabbit pie day.
                So every Friday, that ever comes along
                I get up early
                And sing this little song

                Run, rabbit, run, rabbit,
                Run, run, run.
                Run, rabbit, run, rabbit,
                Run, run, run.
                Bang! Bang! Bang! Bang!
                Goes the farmer's gun
                Run, rabbit, run, rabbit,
                Run, run, run.

                Run, rabbit, run, rabbit,
                Run, run, run.
                Don't give the farmer
                His fun, fun, fun
                He'll get by without his rabbit pie
                So, run, rabbit, run, rabbit,
                Run, run, run.

Boys 2   Run, rabbit, run, rabbit,
Boys   Run,
All   From Farmer Giles.
Boys 1   Rabbit, run, rabbit,
All   Run for miles and miles.
B and G 2   Rabbit, run, rabbit,
All   Run.
B and G 1   Rabbit, run, rabbit,
All   Run, rabbit, run, rabbit
                Run, run, run

Boys	**Girls**
Run, rabbit, run, (Run, rabbit, run)	Run, rabbit,
Run, rabbit, run, (Run, rabbit, run)	Run, rabbit,
Run, rabbit, run, (Run, rabbit, run)	Run, run, run.
(Run), run, run.	
Run, rabbit, run, (Run, rabbit, run)	Run, rabbit,
Run, rabbit, run, (Run, rabbit, run)	Run, rabbit,
Run, rabbit, run, (Run, rabbit, run)	Run, run run.
(Run), run, run.	

All Bang! Bang! Bang! Bang!
Goes the farmer's gun.

Boys   **Girls**
Run, rabbit, run, (Run, rabbit, run)   Run, rabbit,
Run, rabbit, run, (Run, rabbit)   Run, rabbit,
Run from farmer Giles, run a   Run, run,
Hundred miles.   Run.
Take a tip'n

Run, rabbit, run, (Run, rabbit, run)   Run, rabbit,
Run, rabbit, run, (Run, rabbit, run)   Run, rabbit,
Run, rabbit, run, (Run, rabbit, run)   Run, run, run.
(Run), run, run.

Run, rabbit, run, (Run, rabbit, run)   Don't give the
Run, rabbit, pie? (Run, rabbit)   Farmer his
Run.   Fun.

All Ha, Ha, Ha
Ah, Ha, Ha, Ha
He'll get by without his rabbit pie
So,

Boys   **Girls**
Run, rabbit, run, (Run, rabbit, run)   Run, rabbit,
(Run, rabbit,) Run, rabbit,   Run, rabbit,

All Run, run, run, run,
Run, run, run, run,
Run, rabbit, run, rabbit,
Run, rabbit, run, rabbit,
Run, rabbit, run, rabbit,
Run, run, run!

Jeeps cues applause. "Run, Rabbit, Run" play off music

As Wilf and Bultitude share an exchange SR, *we shift to the wings*

Wilf (*during change*) Why Farmer Giles, that's a nice pig you've got there…

Jeeps — oink oink effect

Act II, Scene 6

Bultitude (*as Farmer Giles*) It's that nice I'm going to keep it in the house.
Wilf What about the smell?
Bultitude Oh the pig'll have to get used to that!

As they go

You keep a chicken don't you?
Wilf Indeed I do, and it's going for a song.
Bultitude Where?
Wilf Right over 'ere! ...

They exit

Into pre-record of "Hey Little Hen" off stage, held under after completed scene change

Scene 6

Olive and Sammy are in the wings/dressing room. There is a table with a mirror and prompt telephone. Olive is attending to her make-up. Sammy is desperate to talk

Sammy Ol. Can I have a word with you?
Olive What! Now?
Sammy Don't worry. Wilf's good for three minutes or so ...

Olive turns to face him

Olive All right. What do you want to talk about?
Sammy If ever a line was designed to kill conversation ... (*A beat*) Show's going well tonight, isn't it?
Olive Yes.
Sammy The Grovs are in good voice.
Olive Lovely.
Sammy Young Jeeps is doing us proud.
Olive He always does.
Sammy Amy looks divine.
Olive As always.
Sammy Wilf's sober.
Olive Yes.
Sammy And as for Bultitude ...
Olive Sammy. If you've got something to say, say it, only please don't babble.
Sammy All right. (*Deep breath*) Do I make you happy, Ol?

Olive What?
Sammy I mean it. Are you happy with me?
Olive Sammy this is not the time for this kind of conversation.
Sammy We live together, work together, and yet we never really see each other. At least, I never see you.
Olive Have you been talking to Wilf?
Sammy This has nothing to do with him. Olive, you are without a doubt the best thing that's ever happened to me, but if you want to go back to him, I — I won't stand in your way.
Olive You won't...
Sammy No. Especially if you go back by train.
Olive And who is "him"?
Sammy Gary. I'm not blind you know, Ol.
Olive No, but you're up to something.
Sammy No! Can't you see that I'm trying to do something decent for once in my life? I've forgotten how to make you happy but if you think he can then you mustn't mind me — just go!
Olive I don't know what to say.
Sammy I hope it doesn't work of course. I hope you'll be at each others' throats in a week.
Olive You're serious aren't you?
Sammy Yes.
Olive I don't know what to say. I don't know whether to cry or slap your face.
Sammy I vote cry. My face is my fortune — which means I owe my bookie two ears and a nostril.
Olive You must want me an awful lot to be willing to let me go.
Sammy (*dead serious*) Want, and love, and need.

They embrace. He gets down on his knees

> Let's go down to Brighton after the show — like in the old days. The moment the curtain comes down let's just off without a word! We can watch them laying mines on the beach. Just you and me.

She hesitates. He smooches her some more

> Say yes — well?

Olive I'm thinking about it.

Sammy gets up off his knees

Sammy For heaven's sake woman, if I was any more romantic, I'd be a girl!
Olive So much for sweet talk.

Act II, Scene 6

Sammy I'm sorry love, I didn't mean it. I'm tired, say yes. Please?

Olive is about to say yes, when the prompt corner phone flashes. She answers it

Olive Bultitude? He's on …

Sammy signals "no"

He's busy, can I take a message? … I see — Yes — I'll be sure to tell him. Goodbye. (*She hangs up. Her manner ice cold*) Aren't you going to ask me who that was?
Sammy No.
Olive That, Sammy, was the Home Office, instructing Bultitude to stop the show and they will put on mood music. *Now*! You forgot didn't you? After all the warning and all the threats you forgot to return the bloody security clearance!
Sammy Really, Olive, I am a profess ——

Wilf sticks his head around the door — waving the green form

Wilf Here Sammy. What should I do with this?
Sammy Thanks Wilf. Look Olive, I can explain.
Olive So can I. Your incompetence has finally got this show cancelled! For good.
Sammy So I've ruffled a few feathers, and I'll get yelled at, but we'll be all right, we've all got contracts.
Olive Contracts? Thank you Neville Chamberlain! "I have in my hand a piece of paper". What's next Sammy? Peace in our time?

Bultitude enters

Bultitude Shhhhhhhh. We can hear you, you know.
Olive Mr Bultitude, the Home Office just called. You've got to stop the show.
Bultitude Yes, I thought this might happen.
Olive You mean you knew?
Bultitude Of course. I am the show's producer. Now, I must think. (*He sits and adopts a Rodin position*)
Olive Sammy, what's going on?
Sammy It's all right. He's on our side. What are you going to do?
Bultitude (*looking up*) Ah-ha!

The prompt corner light above his head goes on

I've got it! They're worried about counter propaganda. So we must counter with counter-counter propaganda!
Sammy Will they understand that in Whitehall?
Wilf Why not? It's gibberish.
Bultitude We'll go over their heads! If we can grab the sympathy of America by showing them what it's like over here, perhaps even make them consider entering the war, we may have a chance. This is a job for one man, and one man alone!
Wilf You mean — Sammy?
Bultitude No — I was hoping America might enter the war on *our* side. So I mean — Gary Strong!

Sammy and Wilf flinch

He's a movie star, they'll trust him. Where's Gary Strong!

Jeeps and Amy enter

Jeeps Sammy! The Grovs have nearly finished!
Sammy OK, Olive and Mr Bultitude, you go on ...
Olive What and busk it?
Amy No, no, I've an idea!

Amy whispers into Bultitude's ear as they exit

Sammy Jeeps, wait. Gary's gone to the station. Catch him. Bring him back.
Jeeps What?
Sammy Never mind "what", he can't have got far, run, run ...
Jeeps OK Sammy.

He exits

Sammy And Jeeps ...

Jeeps re-enters

Hurry!

Jeeps exits

We scene change back to the stage

Scene 7

No. 16: All for the Love of a Lady

Grosv. Girls	He loves those eyes of blue He's gone crazy too All for the love of a lady.
Olive	Why do fellows you've known a long while All go potty for some lady's smile? I knew one chap, a good sort of lad
Bultitude	(*very English*) Gee! It's too bad
Grosvenors	Now he's gone mad.
Olive	He became a well-dressed man On the weekly payment plan
Olive **Grosv. Girls**	All for the love of a lady.
Bultitude	And I've bought a Woolworth tie And an eye glass for my eye
Bultitude **Grosvenors**	All for the love of a lady.
Olive	To think that great big gawk Has acquired a fancy walk And he's talking baby talk
Bultitude	Like "poodgy, coodgy, woodgy."
Olive	He has bought a sky blue shirt
Bultitude	Just to match her sky blue skirt
All	All for the love of a lady.
Olive **Grosv. Girls**	He's a bad man A very bad man
All	But he likes his lady love.
Olive	*Il travaille tous les jours* *Il travaille tous les soirs*
All	Oll fur zer lurv of zer laydee
Bultitude	And he combs and combs his hair Till there isn't any there
Bultitude **Grosvenors**	All for the love of a lady.
Olive	*Caressé par la brise* *Avis gît en bien soumise*

Grosvenors	*Mine aurons des choses exquises*
	"Je t'aime, Coco, je t'adore."
	And he's washed behind his ears
Boys	Which he hasn't done for years
All	Oll fur zer lurv of zer laydee.
Bultitude	Lady you're a darling
	A darling a darling
	Lady you're a darling
Band	And so say all the boys!
All	All the fellows in this band
	Go to work and think it's grand
Band	All for the love of a lady
All	You can hear them wail for miles
	Singing theme songs on the tiles
	All for the love
Band	Heavens above!
All	All for the love of a lady.

As the number finishes Jeeps and Gary enter at the back US, *covered in ash and brick dust. Jeeps in particular looks a fine mess*

Sammy steps up to the microphone

Sammy Well b's and g's, Jimmy Cut Glass Diamond there, with the fabulous Grosvenors and of course our own Olive James. But now for something very special. Earlier on you who heard those two tantalizing twins of temptation Olive James and Amy Chapman singing *There's Something About A Soldier*, and that's certainly true of our next guest. You've heard him sing, you've heard him joke, now let's see what he's got to say for himself. Ladies and gentlemen, please welcome Gary Strong!

Bultitude (*aside*) Mr Strong. You must convince the United States what it's like over here. And remember you're speaking to Americans, don't go for their minds — go for their hearts …

Gary walks quietly up to the microphone. The stage darkens until he's held in a spot

Gary Hello America. Hello everybody in the armed forces. Gary Strong here. Or perhaps I should say Pilot Officer Strong of His Majesty's Royal Air Force. If I sound unrehearsed, I am. I had a script but I threw it away. The reason I threw it away is because it cast me in a role I don't deserve,

Act II, Scene 7

that of the conquering hero. I didn't mind playing those parts in the movies — but once you get here and see what's going on with your own eyes, you realize what it means to be brave in the world today.

In America I always listened to Edward R Murrow, and I remember him saying you can't describe the blitz and he's right. You can't. All I can do is give you my impressions. The first thing I noticed was the planes. I hadn't realized you could hear the engines so clearly, it's like a great dark freeway in the sky. I didn't know it would be so bright — that the fires from the docks would light up the horizon, like a sunset bleeding into the Thames. Above all I hadn't realized the extent of the blast the bombs make when they explode. It's not just the noise, though that in itself is terrible. It's that you can feel the ground shuddering beneath your feet with each impact. Later I saw what happens when one of these bombs reaches its target.

At the end of Piccadilly Circus stood a five-storey building — maybe an office, maybe a block of flats, it was hard to tell with the flames and smoke shooting hundreds of feet up into the night sky. A few seconds later the building collapsed, like an old man falling to his knees and I — I just stood there, frozen and helpless, unaware of the miracle to follow. For out of the chaos came the sound of bells, hundreds of bells clanging furiously and a livery tore past me at full tilt. And then another. From the glare of the flames, I could just make out the names on the side of the engines — The Winchester Fire Brigade, The Sheffield Fire Brigade, then one from Bournemouth, then Brighton. From all over the country they'd come, to kill the fires and help keep London alive for another day.

Then suddenly a wall collapsed and a fireman was knocked to the ground. His hose lashed about furiously as I and a young passer-by dragged the unconscious man to safety. Then to my amazement, the young passer-by, despite wearing spectacles thicker than plate glass, leapt at the thrashing hose, and with no thought for his own safety, did his best to play it on the fire. He didn't stop the fire. He didn't win the war. But he did his best.

Everyone onstage now looks at Jeeps. Although affected, Jeeps is still doing his job. He gives Gary the winding up signal

In closing I have to say that the only thing harder to describe than the blitz is the feeling you get over here — the feeling that overnight a nation has turned into a family, side by side, doing their best for the things they love, and discovering within themselves quite remarkable reserves of courage. This is a people's war, but only now have I begun to realize what that means.

There is a beat of silence. Everyone is moved. Wilf gently leads Amy to the microphone to softly sing ——

No. 17: I'm Sending My Blessings

Amy My love for you is deep and true,
An ever burning flame
My heart's aglow, you ought to know
I'll always be the same.

I'm sending my blessings
With every letter I pen
I hope and pray that one fine day
You're in my arms again.

I'm sending my blessings
I know whatever I do
A bluebird sings
Then spreads its wings
And flies from me to you.

It bears a tender message
Wherever you may be
Soon I know my bluebird
Will bring you back to me.

I'm sending my blessings
I pray that heaven above
Will bless you too
When I send you
My blessings and my love

Grosvenors It bears a tender message
Wherever you may be
Soon I know my bluebird
Will bring you back to me.

Amy I'm sending my blessings
I pray that heaven above
Will bless you too
When I send you
My blessings and my love.

Act II, Scene 7   75

Jeeps cues applause. Sammy takes position by the microphone and wraps up

Sammy (*surprisingly gentle*) Well b's and g's, what a day we've had here at the spa. But it's time now to douse the lamp and say goodbye. So until next week, this is Sammy Shaw, telling you to wrap up warm, look after your folks, and whatever happens — keep your chin up!

Jeeps — Door opening effect

Bultitude (*as the Colonel*) Did somebody say gin up?
Sammy Later Colonel, later. 'Till next week gang ...

No. 18: A Song of Tomorrow

Sammy	Skies are clearing		
	Clouds disappearing		
	Now it's up to you		
	This is what you do.		
All	Cheer up and sing		
	A song of tomorrow		
	Tomorrow will be a great day		
Principals	Let the rafters all ring	**Grosvenors**	(*Mmm*)
	Let everyone sing		
All	A song of tomorrow		
	To banish your sorrow		
	Sing a song of tomorrow today!		

Jeeps cues applause. The red light goes off, as the green light goes on. The show's over. They did it! The band starts packing up. Everyone celebrates, talking simultaneously

Daisy We made it!
Irene Well done Sammy!
Wilf Well done all of us!
Sammy Even, and I hate to admit this, even the band were good!
Bultitude Where are they going?

A musician starts collecting band parts, Gary autographs a few

Wilf To the pub. They're musicians. But as for you Mr B, what can I say other than — a star is born!

All agree

Bultitude Well really, I mean to say — Gosh.
Sammy But the important thing is, Heathcliffe, did you have fun tonight?
Bultitude Oh it was more than fun. I mean you start off all nervous and excited, then the show starts and a sort of tingly sensation takes over, and then you start enjoying yourself, and the tingly sensation builds and builds and builds until you feel like you're going to explode! Do you ever get that?
Sammy Yes, but rarely in front of an audience.

Jeeps comes on

Jeeps Mr Bultitude, telephone. It's the Home Office, BBC.

Everyone freezes

Bultitude Wish me luck!
Sammy Do you think you can pull it off?
Bultitude Who knows. But thanks to Mr Strong here, we have a fighting chance!

Bultitude exits

Sammy (*suddenly barking*) Jeeps!

Jeeps jumps nervously. Sammy's kidding. Sammy takes Jeeps' hand

Well done son, I'm really proud of you.

They all gather around

Andrew We're all proud of you.
Wilf You're a regular Gunga Din!
Daisy A hero!
Simon On both sides of the Atlantic.
Jeeps It was nothing, really. Anyone would've done the same.

Amy approaches

Amy Excuse me Jeeps ...

She takes him to one side. They sit. She cleans his face with her handkerchief

Does it hurt?

Act II, Scene 7   77

Jeeps No, no, no, no, Ouch!
Amy Sorry.
Jeeps It's all right.
Amy Are you sure. They're right you know, you are a hero, Jeeps.
Jeeps You think so?
Amy And the best kind. A quiet hero. (*She takes off his glasses*) Why Mr Jeeps — you're handsome!
Jeeps Amy, you will — will you go out with me? Did you hear me, I said, will you …

She kisses him. Everyone has been watching and applauds

Bultitude enters, looking serious

Sammy Well?
Bultitude Well, the Home Office was furious. Apoplectic!
Olive Oh no …
Bultitude However, the Americans loved it! Consequently it's been decided your propaganda value outweighs your monumental incompetence! You may live! But …

Everybody freezes

Heads must roll. Uncleared material has been broadcast, and unauthorized, and uncleared personnel have appeared on a transmission. Somebody must pay with their job. (*He looks at Sammy*)

General horror

I have managed to persuade the authorities that there is one person responsible, through inexperience, and lack of observance of procedural processes. The shoulders that must bear this responsibility and blame (*gravely*) will never again work for the BBC. (*Pause*) Jimmy Cut Glass Diamond will never perform for the corporation again. His career is over.

Relief all round. Wilf hugs Bultitude

Wilf You star!
Sammy Thanks Heathcliffe.
Bultitude No, no, thank Mr Strong.
Olive He's right, you were extraordinary, Gary. But why on earth did you go up top again?
Gary Didn't Wilf give you my message?

Olive No.
Gary Oh. I was on my way to the station. I got word to report immediately.

Sammy steps in, and tries to edge Gary off stage

Sammy Well, we all owe you a debt of gratitude that I can hardly put into words. So I won't. Bye.
Gary Still, it's curious you know. Now that I've had a chance to look this over, I can't make it out ...

Sammy continues trying to show him out

Sammy Oh, I'm sure they know that they're doing. Read it on the way.

Gary takes out the telegram

Gary It says I'm to report to "Whinge Commander Foxley" of the "Royal Air Farce, Scapa Flow, Scotland."
Sammy What's wrong with that?
Gary Well, apart from the spelling mistakes, it's a naval base.
Olive Say that again ...
Gary It's a naval base ...
Olive Before that ...
Gary Apart from the spelling mistakes ...
Olive (*taking the telegram*) I knew it! I knew it! Wilf — Wilf!
Wilf You screamed, madam?
Olive You did this, didn't you?
Sammy Now Olive, calm down ...
Olive And to think I fell for it! (*To Sammy*) I actually believed you were prepared to let me go, simply to make me happy!
Sammy What do you think I am — an idiot?
Gary You mean this isn't real?
Olive Nothing's real around here, Gary. I'm sorry.
Sammy Olive, please, wait. Look — if you'd gone off with him you'd have been miserable. Maybe not today. Maybe not tomorrow — but soon, and for the rest of your life!
Olive Oh I see! So you did it for me?
Sammy Yes.
Olive Thank you. Thank you so much. *Unbelievable*!

She pushes past him

Sammy Well, p'raps not entirely for you. There was a smidgin of self interest — maybe even a tad. (*To Gary*) Is a tad bigger than a smidgin?

Act II, Scene 7

He sees Olive is nearly off stage

> All right! I did it for me! Olive — I was scared.

She stops

> For the first time in my life I could imagine you gone, and and — I couldn't take that chance. I meant everything I said before. Without you I'm nothing. I love you Olive.
>
> **Olive** If only you knew the meaning of the word.

Accompanied by only the piano, Sammy sings

No. 19: My Thanks to You

Sammy
Words have such wonderful meaning
When they're sincere and they're true
Mine surely are
Too humble by far
But these little words
Are just for you …

For all you mean to me
My thanks to you
For every memory
My thanks to you
My thanks for everything
We love to share
For all the joy you bring
When you are there.

These foolish words of mine
Could never say
How slow the hands of time
When you're away
As years go rolling by
My whole life through
I give my love and all
My thanks to you.

They kiss

Gary has realized the truth — Sammy loves Olive and vice versa

Olive You're such a chump, Sammy Shaw. You couldn't even get this right could you? You needed to fake a telegram, so who did you get to write it? The only man in the country who spells "London" with a "U".
Sammy I need you Ol. Always have done. Always will.
Olive I know. (*She turns to Gary*) Look Gary I — I ...
Gary (*embracing her warmly*) If you need a best man, let me know.
Sammy Thanks Gary.
Olive You will take care of yourself won't you?
Gary Hey — I'll be fine. Selznick won't let me die — I got three pictures left on my contract.

He moves US, *and autographs a puzzled Sophie's script*

   Here you are.
Sophie Thank you.

Gary exits

Sammy Here Ol — About what Gary just said, what do you think?
Olive What?
Sammy You know, shall we, like, in the funny clothes, go down the whatsit, with the ...
Olive What?
Sammy You know — bann the posts — you and me — plight our trowels to each other — in one of those big — stone — religious places?
Olive Sammy, why don't you just ask me to marry you?
Sammy I'm-doing-it, I'm-doing-it!

They celebrate, as the rest join in for the finale

No. 20: A Song of Tomorrow (Reprise)

Sammy	Skies are clearing
Olive	Clouds disappearing
Wilf (*to Olive*)	Now it's up to you
Sammy	⎱ This is what you do.
Olive	⎰

Full Company	Cheer up and sing
	A song of tomorrow
	Tomorrow will be a great day
	Let the rafters all ring (*Mmm*)
	Let everyone sing

Act II, Scene 7

                A song of tomorrow today
                (Let ev'rybody sing that)

                There's gonna be
                A brighter tomorrow
                Already it's well on the way
                There's the sun breaking through (*Ooh*)
                It's telling you to sing
                A song of tomorrow
                Today.

Wilf
Jeeps   We've been in the doldrums
Bultitude We've been in the dumps

Gary   Get out of the doldrums
            Here comes happiness
Bultitude In big large lumps.

Olive   There's gonna be
Sammy A brighter tomorrow
            Already it's well on the way
            There's the sun breaking through
            It's telling you to (*Mmm*)
            Sing a song of tomorrow today.

All   We've been in the doldrums
            We've been in the dumps
            Get out of the doldrums
            Here comes happiness
            In big large lumps.

            Cheer up and sing
            Cheer up and sing
            Cheer up and sing
            A song (of tomorrow)
            Tomorrow will be a great day
            Let the rafters all ring
            Let everyone sing
            A song of tomorrow today
            Sing a song of tomorrow today!

No. 21: The Calls

Run, Rabbit, Run

Grosvenors	Run, rabbit, run, rabbit, Run, run, run, Run, rabbit, run, rabbit, Run, run, run. Bang! Bang! Bang! Bang! Bang! Goes the farmer's gun, so Run, rabbit, run, rabbit, Run, run, run.

Who's Been Polishing the Sun?

All	Who's been polishing the sun? Rubbing out the clouds of grey They must have known (just) how I like it
Sammy	Everything
All	Everything
Sammy	Everything
All	Everything Everything's coming my way.

FURNITURE AND PROPERTY LIST

ACT I

On stage: Prop baskets. *In them*: costumes
Rehearsal piano. *On it*: song sheet music, ukulele
Piano stool
Tea urn, tea cups, jug of water, glasses etc.
Chairs
Ventriloquist's doll
Paper
Microphones
Telephone
Music stands
Clock
Sound Effects Table. *On it*: telephone, motor horn, selection of "Applause" signs (more applause, etc.), coconuts, tins of pebbles, trays with gravel and sand, vibraslap, bells, whistles, gongs and other devices to create the following sound effects: countryside noises; chickens, cows, sheep, pigs. Miniature door for; knocking, creaking, opening, closing effects. Thwack effect. Slapping. Screaming. Footsteps receding. Cracking knuckles. Boing effect. Whizz siren. Tweet, tweet. Saw noise. Eek. Noisy crash. Gun shot.

Offstage: Script (**Sammy**)
Song sheets (**Sammy**)
Book of guidelines; a green, soft-covered pamphlet (**Bultitude**)
Script (**Wilf**)

Personal: **Bultitude**: watch (worn throughout)
Jeeps: spectacles and watch (worn throughout)
Sammy: green security clearance form and pen
Gary: pen
Simon: half-a-crown
Wilf: notepaper and pen
Irene: note
Bultitude: green security clearance form
Amy: handkerchief

ACT II

Scene 1

On stage: Chair
Small table. *On it*: mirror, prompt phone (with red light)

Personal: **Gary**: packet of cigarettes and box of matches
Olive: matches

Scene 2

Set: Prop table

Strike: Chair
Small table. *On it* mirror, prompt phone

Personal: **Wilf**: flask of Brandy

Scene 3

Set: Microphones

Strike: Prop table

Personal: **Amy**: letters

Scene 4

On stage: As before

Scene 5

Offstage: Bundle of letters, phone numbers etc. (**Wilf**)
Telegram (**Wilf**)
Prop telephone (**Wilf**)

Scene 6

On stage: Chair
Small table. *On it* mirror, prompt phone, **Olive**'s make-up

Scene 7

On stage: As before

Strike: Chair
Small table. *On it* mirror, prompt phone, **Olive**'s make-up

LIGHTING PLOT

Practical fittings required: green and red studio lights and "On Air" sign above sound effects table. Interior. The same throughout

ACT I

To open:	Bring up general overall lighting	
Cue 1	**Wilf**: "*Shawwwwwww!*" *Spotlight on* SR	(Page 3)
Cue 2	The music stops *The spotlight wanders around the stage finally alighting on a doorway at the back of the stage*	(Page 3)
Cue 3	**Bultitude** enters *Cut spot*	(Page 3)
Cue 4	**Amy**: "Thank you." *The lights change*	(Page 14)
Cue 5	**Jeeps** returns **Amy** to **Gary** *Lights return to general effect*	(Page 15)
Cue 6	As music hall back cloth comes in *Lights change to music hall-style. Bring up spot on* **Gary**	(Page 23)
Cue 7	The backcloth is removed *Cut spot. Return to general lighting*	(Page 25)
Cue 8	**Bultitude** and **Amy** exit *Lights fade to black-out. When ready bring up general lighting*	(Page 29)
Cue 9	They lead **Bultitude** off *Fade to black-out. When ready bring up general lighting front of tabs. Green light on*	(Page 32)
Cue 10	The CURTAIN rises *Bring up general lighting. Snap off green light. Snap on red light and "On Air" sign*	(Page 36)

Cue 11	**Bultitude**: "Thank you." *Fade to black-out*	(Page 45)

ACT II

To open:	Bring up wings lighting effect	
Cue 12	**Olive**: (*singing*) "I may find out some day." *Cross-fade to* **Sammy** *in another area of stage (f.o.t)*	(Page 49)
Cue 13	To open Scene 3 *Snap off green studio light. Snap on red light and "On Air" sign. Bring up overall general lighting*	(Page 51)
Cue 14	Pre-record of "Hey Little Hen" *Cross-fade to wings lighting effect*	(Page 67)
Cue 15	**Sammy**: "Please?" *Prompt corner phone flashes*	(Page 69)
Cue 16	**Olive** picks up the phone *Cut phone flash*	(Page 69)
Cue 17	**Gary** walks up to the microphone *The stage darkens. Spotlight on* **Gary**	(Page 72)
Cue 18	**Amy**: (*singing*) "My blessings and my love." *Cut spot. Bring up general lighting*	(Page 74)
Cue 19	**Jeeps** cues applause *Red light goes off. Green light goes on*	(Page 75)

EFFECTS PLOT

ACT I

Cue 1	As music hall back cloth comes in *Audience noise effect*	(Page 23)
Cue 2	**Gary**: "Johnson and James!" *Audience applause*	(Page 23)
Cue 3	**Gary** and **Olive**: (*singing*) "… one more." *Audience effect continues*	(Page 24)
Cue 4	**Both**: (*singing*) "… just one more." *Audience applause effect*	(Page 25)
Cue 5	**Sammy**: "— that will be all." *Air raid sirens*	(Page 40)
Cue 6	**Gary**: (*singing*) "As badly as it ever could be." (2nd time) *Air raid starts in the background gradually increasing in volume*	(Page 42)
Cue 7	**All**: (*singing*) "Everything's coming my way!" (last time) *Boom! Massive explosion detonates nearby*	(Page 45)

ACT II

To open:	Air raid continues. Bomb drops close by	
Cue 8	**Olive**: "Thanks." *Bomb explodes nearby*	(Page 47)
Cue 9	**Wilf**: "Story of my life!" *Bomb in distance*	(Page 48)
Cue 10	**Jeeps** enters *The all-clear sounds*	(Page 50)
Cue 11	**Wilf**: "Right over 'ere!…" *Pre-record of* Hey Little Hen *offstage. Cut when scene change is completed*	(Page 67)

The actor playing **Jeeps** produces many of the sound effects in this play from his sound effects table on stage. He is also responsible for prompting audience applause. The cues are listed below. (* indicates the cue may be provided by the drummer)

Cue 1	**Wilf**: "... my name's Wilfred Davies." *Honk*	(Page 33)
Cue 2	**Olive** enters **Jeeps** *holds up "Applause" sign*	(Page 33)
Cue 3	**Olive**: "He's a burglar." **Drum crash*	(Page 33)
Cue 4	**Amy** enters **Jeeps** *holds up "Applause" sign*	(Page 34)
Cue 5	**Wilf**: "... Cut Glass Diamond!" **Jeeps** *holds up "Applause" sign*	(Page 34)
Cue 6	**Wilf**: "... Shaw!" **Jeeps** *cues applause*	(Page 35)
Cue 7	**All**: (*singing*) "Hello to the sun." **Jeeps** *cues applause*	(Page 35)
Cue 8	**All**: (*singing*) "... let the people sing!" **Jeeps** *cues applause*	(Page 37)
Cue 9	**Wilf**: "... Hope Springs Health Spa —" *Countryside noises, chickens, cows, sheep*	(Page 37)
Cue 10	**Sammy**: "... willow on leather." *Thwack*	(Page 37)
Cue 11	**Sammy**: "Open the door, Wilf..." *Creeakk!*	(Page 38)
Cue 12	**Sammy**: "What sound?" *Screams/slaps*	(Page 38)
Cue 13	**Sammy**: "... Gracie Fields tuning up." *Louder screams/slaps*	(Page 38)
Cue 14	**Sammy**: "... in for a massage." *Footsteps on gravel tray — receding*	(Page 38)
Cue 15	**Sammy**: "Well — here goes ..." *Knock, knock. Door opening*	(Page 38)

Cue 16	**Sammy**: "… we won't be interrupted." *Door opening*	(Page 39)
Cue 17	**Bultitude**: "Well, toodle-pip." *Door shutting*	(Page 39)
Cue 18	**Sammy**: "Should have stayed the night." *Cracking*	(Page 39)
Cue 19	**Bultitude**: "… and we'll begin …" *Slapping*	(Page 39)
Cue 20	**Sammy**: "… rather attached to my body." *Boing*	(Page 39)
Cue 21	**Sammy**: "— leave that alone." *Boing. Door opening*	(Page 39)
Cue 22	**Sammy**: "A-ha the French resistance!" *Door shutting. Slapping*	(Page 40)
Cue 23	**Bultitude**: "… like a coiled spring." *Boing*	(Page 40)
Cue 24	Air raid sirens *Door opening*	(Page 40)
Cue 25	**Wilf**: "Boss, I'm gone." *Whizz siren*	(Page 40)
Cue 26	**Sammy**: "… that gas masked man?" *Whizz siren*	(Page 40)
Cue 27	**Wilf**: "And look who I've brought …" *Door opening*	(Page 41)
Cue 28	**Sammy**: "… Mr Gary Strong!" **Jeeps** *holds up "Applause" card. Door opening*	(Page 41)
Cue 29	**Olive**: "… a care in the world." *Tweet, tweet*	(Page 41)
Cue 30	**Gary**: (*singing*) "Oh Buddy I'm in love." **Jeeps** *cues applause*	(Page 42)
Cue 31	**All**: (*singing*) "… coming my way!" **Jeeps** *cues applause*	(Page 44)

ACT II

Cue 32	**Grosvenors**: *(singing)* "… of the grand cavalcade!" **Jeeps** *cues applause*	(Page 53)
Cue 33	**Sammy**: "… a gander." *Drum crash	(Page 54)
Cue 34	**Sammy**: "… next port of call …" *Door opening*	(Page 54)
Cue 35	**Sammy**: "… under mifireplace." *Drum crash	(Page 54)
Cue 36	**Sammy**: "… for complete silence." *Drum roll	(Page 54)
Cue 37	**Sammy**: "… a man drumming." *Drum stops	(Page 54)
Cue 38	**Wilf**: "Thank you Mr Shaw." *Saw noise. Boing. Eek. Noisy crash*	(Page 55)
Cue 39	**Sammy**: "… Miss Amy Chapman!" **Jeeps** *holds up "Applause" sign*	(Page 55)
Cue 40	Ali Baba's Camel *Sound effects throughout (as p. 61)*	(Page 61)
Cue 41	**All**: *(singing)* "His camels gone to…" *Honk.* **Jeeps** *cues applause*	(Page 63)
Cue 42	**Sammy**: "… one hump or two!" *Bang bang! (Clappers)*	(Page 63)
Cue 43	**Bultitude**: "Can I pay with this?" *Cluck cluck!*	(Page 63)
Cue 44	**Sammy**: "… personal chicks!" *Drum crash	(Page 64)
Cue 45	**Bultitude**: "There he goes!" *Boing boing!*	(Page 64)
Cue 46	**All**: "Run, run, run!" **Jeeps** *cues applause*	(Page 66)

Cue 47	**Wilf**: "… you've got there …" *Oink oink*	(Page 66)
Cue 48	**All**: (*singing*) "… for the love of a lady." **Jeeps** *cues applause*	(Page 72)
Cue 49	**Amy**: (*singing*) " … and my love." **Jeeps** *cues applause*	(Page 74)
Cue 50	**Sammy**: "— keep your chin up!" *Door opening*	(Page 75)
Cue 51	**All**: (*singing*) "… tomorrow today!" **Jeeps** *cues applause*	(Page 75)